MW01141609

Body of Athenian General, Phocian, being carried out of Athens in the 4th century B.C. He was put to death on false charges of treason then cremated as extra punishment. Painting by Nicolas Poussin done in 1648. [Courtesy of National Museum of Wales on loan from the Earl of Plymouth, UK].

Better to Bury Than to Burn

by
Ian T. Taylor

TFE
PUBLISHING

Copyright © 2002 by Ian T. Taylor

Canadian Cataloguing in Publication Data
Taylor, Ian T. 1931-
Better to Bury than to Burn
Bibliography: p. 130
Includes Index
ISBN 0-969-1788-7-5
1. Cremation—Religious aspects—Christianity
2. Cremation—Biblical teaching. 1. Title.
BT826.4.T39 2002   236'.1   C2002 – 900726-7

All rights reserved. No part of this publication
may be reproduced, stored in a retrieval system,
or transmitted in any form or by any means,
electronic, mechanical, photocopying, recording,
or otherwise, without prior permission in writing
from the publisher except for brief quotations
for inclusion in a magazine, newspaper, or broadcast.

All quotations from the NKJV
Except where otherwise noted

Editorial: CVC Editing
Design: TFE Graphics
Typesetting and Scanning: The Right Type
Printed in Canada by: AGMV MARQUIS

TFE PUBLISHING

US	CANADA
P.O. Box 48220	33 Ontario St., Suite 112
Minneapolis, MN 55433	Kingston, ON K7L 5E3
Tel/Fax: (763) 856-3989	Tel/Fax: (613) 541-3925/6

Table of Contents

Acknowledgements

Asking trusted friends who have had the advantage of spending many years with Scripture can be helpful in understanding some of those difficult passages. Nevertheless, none of us can escape the fact that we all come to Scriptural understanding with a whole baggage of presuppositions. Often, these consist of what we think was said by certain passages rather than what was actually written. After a few years of repeating these versions to others, our minds can become gospel-hardened and this was often how tradition eventually became established as church dogma. Protestants are generally willing to acknowledge that this has happened in the Roman Catholic church but fail to realize that a similar thing has happened in their own denominations. Scientists are very much aware that bias on the part of the researcher can cause him to see what he wants to see. Even so and with a sincere approach, bias still has a major influence on the scientist's search for the truth. How then can we find the truth? Firstly, we must have a will to believe that the Scriptures in their original tongues are God's truth given to mankind through His inspired writers. Secondly, we accept that God has sovereignly preserved His Words throughout the centuries so that we have them in inerrant form. The translations that most of us read today are really secondary sources since they have passed through the bias of the translators. Scripture is thus our primary source of truth. If we can accept that as human beings, we will inevitably have a bias, we might just as well adopt the bias which we have just agreed to is God's truth. By patient meditation on Scripture and digging into library sources to find out what others have found, God is true to His promise and will reveal His truth to us. The most difficult part is the stumbling block inside our own head!

I want to thank several friends for helpful discussion but first thanks to a well-respected pastor of a large North American evangelical church; both shall be nameless. I had asked him what happens to the Christian when he dies? His answer went something like this: "When a Christian dies, he goes straight to heaven." I nodded and asked, "And the sinner?" "He goes straight to hell." I then asked, "But doesn't the judgment come after the resurrection?" "Ah, you have to understand that that judgment is only a confirmation of the judgment the person receives immediately he dies." Here was the tidy answer from a highly qualified man and, while nothing further was said, he knew as well as I did that this was all complete nonsense. I thanked him and went my way determined to get to the bottom of this quite fundamental question. The fog cleared and the end came in sight only after well over a decade of patient search.

Then thanks to Dr. Harold McCarthy, my good friend of many years, who has studied Hebrew and Greek and taught theology at seminary level. We disagreed on many points but always left as friends. Special thanks to Edward Fudge for his book, *The Fire that Consumes*. This caused me to consider what Scripture really means by "eternal punishment." Finding a copy of LeRoy Froom's two-volume work *The Conditionalist Faith of Our Fathers* was an eye-opener to the disasterous influence of Plato on the Christian Church. Froom's work caused me to read the classic Greek literature and find out what the Greeks had really said. The providential death of another friend, Norman Gowland, an irascible old bachelor who gave me, as executor of his estate, valuable insight into the disposal business. Many thanks also to David S. J. Harris and Tony Costa who diligently read the manuscript and made many valuable comments. Finally, special thanks to Connie Carter who, with beady eye and nimble finger, edited the manuscript. Any remaining errors are, of course, mine.

Preface

This little book was written for the Christian reader. Increasingly, there are those who want to make a responsible attempt to put their house in order before final departure and are faced with the question: "Is it right to be cremated?" The title of the book indicates that it is better to be buried while the text provides the Scriptural reason. However, this is only one facet of a much larger and more important issue that concerns belief in the general resurrection. The sainted Paul pointed out that without belief in the resurrection of the dead the Christian is, of all men, most pitiable. Thus, any attack on this belief must be taken seriously. The importance is reflected by the fact that the grounds for disbelief were laid down in the Garden of Eden. In the next hundred pages or so we will expose and document these tactics step by step. Cremation is just the latest and perhaps most deadly attack in a series to destroy the belief in the resurrection. In the near future we can even expect legislation to make the practice of cremation mandatory.

As with so many social practices that have been adopted by the Christian West in the past couple of centuries, modern cremation was a birthchild of the French Revolution. Organized pressure tactics to promote cremation in Europe, in Great Britain and in North America began in earnest about a century after the Revolution and have been driven by a small but dedicated band of humanists. Today, the practice is well established with approximately half the body disposals in North America by cremation; in Europe and Great Britain the proportion is significantly greater. The reasons given to justify the practice are based upon specious ecological arguments. That is, just as the world is said to be overpopulated, so it is argued that the world is running out of burial space. These arguments are only possible because they appeal to the majority who now live in and seldom leave the inner city and suburbia. A further facet of persuasion is the lower cost of cremation compared to burial. As we shall see, the problem arose in the first place by the unscriptural insistence of disposal in a box rather than by earth burial. From box to coffin to casket, the costs have so escalated that the pagan practice of cremation now appears acceptable.

When asked about cremation, Christians who genuinely want to do the right thing about their final departure, usually reply, "It may be alright for others but it's not for me." If this is the Spirit saying "No" then Scripture should give us the reason. Unfortunately these days, simply asking the busy pastor or priest will seldom provide a satisfying answer. The reply recorded in the Acknowledgement is perhaps more detailed than is usually given; a more typical reply would be, "Why worry? You'll be with Jesus." Others will argue that it is a pagan practice and not the right way to treat a former temple of the Holy Spirit. However, none of these replies are good enough and it would be reasonable to expect that Scripture should give us a clear answer if we are prepared to search for it. The author of Scripture has graciously invited His people to, "Come let us reason together." With patience and a little open-minded searching into Scripture and history, we find that God has indeed provided a sound reason why His people should have have nothing to do with cremation.

The first few chapters are mainly historical and show how and why cremation was introduced and the sources of many common beliefs and customs in the Church. There are likely to be surprises for everyone in these chapters. Along the way it was necessary to make a very brief mention of the chemistry of body decomposition. This is there because it is in this area that the Church began to depart from God's instructions. The later chapters are for those who really want to know what Scripture has to say about cremation and here there may be more surprises. The final chapter is a brief hands-on approach to preparation for departure.

1

How Cremation was Introduced

Why do the heathen rage,
and the people plot a vain thing?
The kings of the earth set themselves,
and the rulers take counsel together,
against the Lord and His Anointed.
HANDEL'S *MESSIAH,* 1742 [PSALM 2:1-2]

What Price Cremation?

Turning points in history are most often pivoted about off-beat characters who seemingly have a single mission; when that mission is complete they take their exit from life and history's stage. Physician William Price (1800–1893) was certainly an off-beat character. It was Price who was responsible for dramatically introducing the pagan practice of cremation into Christian Britain. Price's father was an ordained clergyman in the Church of England but his son, William, had been thoroughly disillusioned by what he had seen of Christianity. As a medical student William Price exceeded all others in the examinations, then became a competant physician, a clever surgeon and established his practice near Pontypridd, South Wales. He was a strident atheist, practicing nudist, studied Hindu mysticism and became a notable Arch Druid. He believed in free love and never married, but during his lifetime lived with several women. He may have gotten away with his beliefs in the obscurity of a large city but he was living in the centre of Welsh revival country![1] The controversy over his life-style was so great that he had to leave the country twice and lived in Paris, but he always came back.

Doctor Price had only one daughter but finally, in his 84th year, a son was born and Price named him Jesus Christ. However, when only five months old the infant died. Ten years earlier, in 1874, a flurry of articles by senior members of the medical profession had appeared in some of the more stuffy Victorian magazines promoting the pratcice of cremation. Sir Henry Thompson had led this

1

crusade by means of a lengthy article in which he addressed every possible objection. The major concern of these medical writers was that the traditional method of body disposal by burial was posing a serious danger to the public health in their tight little island. Opposing articles by the clergy supporting burial gave rather nebulous arguments from Scripture. Undoubtedly, Price saw an opportunity to demonstrate in a practical manner which side of the argument he supported. He built a funeral pyre on the Welsh hillside and attempted to cremate the body of his son. The date was 1884. The police were called, recovered the partially burnt body, there was a court case and much publicity that brought the issue of cremation to the attention of the general public. Essentially, because no one had been cremated in Britain since the Roman occupation there was no law either for or against it. The judge found a precedent from 1635, in the last words of Sir Thomas Browne's *Hydriotaphia,* "... *it matters not whether the body is buried or burnt* ... " and that same quotation is still parroted today in defence of cremation. Marvellously fanning the flames of publicity, Price defended himself dressed in his Druid's robes, lost the case on a technicality, but won the right to finish the cremation of his son. The following year cremation was legalized. Nine years later and at the age of 93, Price himself was cremated on the same Welsh hillside before a crowd of twenty-thousand horrified spectators. The practice of cremation in Britain had arrived and the date was 1893.[2]

To Dust Thou Shalt Return

In the very beginning, before there had been any death, God told Adam that he came from the dust of the ground and that he must return to the dust of the ground:

Genesis 3:19

> In the sweat of your face you shall eat bread till you return to the ground, For out of it you were taken; For dust you are, and to dust you shall return.

Abel's murdered body was returned to the dust of the ground and throughout human history this has been by far the most common method of body disposal. Of course, among the more pagan nations examples can always be found of other methods, some quite bizarre. The Zoroastrians [modern Iran] expose their dead on "towers of silence" as carrion to be eaten by birds, while the Tibetans practice "sky burial" by cutting up their dead then feeding the

Dr. William Price (1800–1893) dressed in full Arch Druid regalia. This is how he was dressed as he presented his own defense at court. He had attempted to cremate his only son whom he had named Jesus Christ. [Welsh Folk Museum, St. Fagans, Cardiff]

pieces to the vultures.[3] Other cultures have employed cremation but the practice has always been confined to the minority mostly because the fuel has usually been too expensive for the common man. The Jew and the Muslim have always kept that early commandment when it is in their power to do so. To this day their practice is to ritually wash, wrap and bury within 24 hours if possible. There was an apparent exception in the case of Christ. The Sabbath began at sunset and left no time for formal burial so His body was placed unburied in a sealed cave with the expectation that washing, wrapping with spices and burial could take place immediately after the Sabbath. However, His Resurrection left no body to bury! For the rest of us it has to be said that the Christian West long ago departed from the commandment to return to the dust. The rationale was often subtle and only becomes apparent when exposed. We shall attempt to do that in this chapter.

At the very core of man's psyche is a desire to impart significance to himself and an unwillingness to accept the finality of death. Preservation of the body by all the arts of the modern funeral establishment is common today but the entire exercise is one of pure vanity, a futile attempt at immortality. In this we are reminded of the first lie in the Garden:

Genesis 2:17

> God to Adam: "… but of the tree of the knowledge of good and evil you shall not eat; for in the day that you eat of it you shall surely die."

Genesis 3:4-5

> And the serpent said to the woman, "You will not surely die…"

Satan is the Father of Lies, and in those words, *"You will not surely die"* is the lying promise of immortality. As we shall see, this lie has profoundly influenced the Christian Church. For many centuries pagans and later Christians, continued to return the body to the earth but then the Western Church permitted the use of the closed box. This is actually non-burial since the body does not return to the dust of the ground as commanded. Non-burial for all of us today, pagans and Christians alike, long ago became the accepted way in the affluent Christian West. This situation has come about step by crafty step. The bottom line is that Christian non-burial has eventually led to disbelief in the resurrection. Cremation only enhances that disbelief. The story is a long one but with the threat to Christianity's key doctrine, it is well worth exposing.

The Chemistry of Decomposition

When bodies are simply wrapped in cloth and buried in suitable soil, they completely return to the dust within ten years, often five. Earth burial has been the practice for the vast majority throughout the history of man and to a large extent still is. Preservation in wooden or even steel boxes, such as we have come to expect in North America, does not have a very long history. The word "casket" is of relatively modern coinage and was introduced to give status and distinguish it from the common coffin. It is nothing more than a fancy and grossly more expensive version of the plain wooden box. The word "coffin" derives from the Greek *kophinos* meaning basket, the same word used in the Biblical account of the loaves and the fishes. Early coffins were, in fact, often baskets and the word "coffin" will more correctly be retained throughout this book. Closed coffin burial was, for most of history, confined to the very wealthy, to royalty, a miniscule proportion of the population. It is for this reason that after thousands of years even a small island like the British Isles is not now one vast cemetery.

The rate of decomposition depends upon the chemistry of the

soil; in some, decomposition is extremely rapid. In contrast, the soil of Egypt is so dry that no decomposition takes place. The preserved though shrunken bodies of the Egyptian poor who were simply wrapped and buried have become "mummified" by natural processes and are still found preserved this way after four-thousand years. As far as the chemistry of decomposition is concerned, earth burial permits the nitrogen in the body to be converted to nitrates that are a beneficial fertilizer whereas in the cremation process the nitrogen is lost to the atmosphere as ammonia.[4] Other noxious products such as carbonic acid gas are also produced during cremation. These air-polluting gases should be of concern to the environmental conservationists but are very seldom, if ever, mentioned.

The decay process under earth burial conditions is really quite amazing as wave after wave of specialist insects enter the body in exactly the right order. They work together [5] and can very efficiently strip a mature man's body to the bone in two months.[6] Forensic science is able to determine rather precisely how long a body has been buried by the insect species present.[7, 8] The use of closed coffins, on the other hand, introduces a completely different chemistry because the insects and the air are excluded. In this case, there is a tendency to preserve the body by the formation of a soapy substance called adipocere; bodies buried under these conditions can last for centuries.[9] Interestingly, while alive it is the blood that sustains our life but once dead it is the blood that hastens the decay process. For this reason when a body has to be transported to another State, Province or country for burial, there are laws in most countries including North America, that make it mandatory to retard the decay process for the safety and comfort of other travellers. This is most commonly done by embalming, a practice that was re-introduced to the Christian West as recently as the 1860s.[10]

History of Body Disposal

In the early periods of the Greek and Roman civilizations disposal was by earth burial. It was only in the later stages when a fear of mutilation of the dead arose that cremation became the chosen and more certain way to go among the wealthy. Roman scholar, Pliny the Elder, tells us in his *Natural History* that cremation was introduced at first by the Greek military as a means of disposing of their own dead.[11] For an army far from home it was not possible to return the dead to their homeland, while to bury on the field would invite subsequent mutilation if the army had to make a hasty retreat.[12] In a battle, time was always set aside by mutual agreement of both sides to clear the dead from the field; the army fighting away from home then built cremation fires to burn their corpses. However, they were careful to ensure that several days elapsed between death and cremation. The Greek poet/historian, Homer in his *Illiad* said ten days,[13] the Roman poet, Virgil in his *Aeneid*, claimed three days.[14] This follows from the early pagan belief that for several days after death the body still had some "life" in it until the soul separated from the body.

Among the Jews at the time of Christ, rabbinical authorities insisted that body disposal consist of a ceremonial wash, wrap in cloth and earth burial "*between four cities*" before sun-down. Neither Jews nor Muslims have ever used coffins or permitted cremation of their own people. Some Bible translations, e.g. the NIV, incorrectly say that Jesus "*touched the coffin*" of the widow of Nain's son (Luke 7:14). However, in the Greek the word *soros* was used, meaning bier. The accepted way was earth burial in pits or cemeteries as far as possible from centers of population, preferably on a hill. This approach sensibly avoided pollution of the city drinking water. To this day, orthodox Jews insist on being returned to the earth. In North America the orthodox Jew has no choice and must use a coffin because local by-laws insist upon it. It is understood, however, that some local authorities will permit six holes to be made in the bottom of the coffin of an orthodox Jew to allow body fluids to return to the earth. At the time of Christ, rabbinical authorities absolutely prohibited burial within walled cities and this fact is at the root of today's scholarly controversy over the authentic site of the Holy Sepulchre in Jerusalem. The Roman Church of the Holy Sepulchre is now well inside the present city wall, but the question is whether the course of the walls at the time of Christ included or excluded the site of Christ's tomb. Protestants generally regard the Garden tomb, just outside the present city wall, as the authentic site.[15]

The early Christians were mostly converted Jews and the practice of earth burial outside the cities was continued. As Christians began to suffer persecution martry's bodies were also buried in the same roadside cemeteries, but their gravesites tended to became centers for prayer. When miraculous healings were associated with the remains of certain martyrs, shrines were erected either at the gravesite or, the remains were removed to a more convenient location. Later, the living then moved in among the dead as the shrines became popular and required maintenance and protection. The persecution in Rome resulted in many thousands of martyrs and these, together with the bodies of wealthy Christians, were laid to rest in the now famous catacombs. Stevenson has shown that contrary to popular misconception these underground tunnels were not sanctuaries for the persecuted faithful but a safe haven for the faithful dead. Roman pagans took delight in mutilating the bodies of Christians and the tunnels could be relatively easy to defend.[16] This method of protection also had the advantage of allowing the living to more conveniently pay their respects to their dead and even have their "last supper" with the dead. However, the catacomb burial was not strictly earth burial since the bodies were placed in stone boxes or in a sealed niche in the rock walls.

The early Christian Church authorities—referred to here as the Latin Church to distinguish it from the Roman Catholic Church that we know today—continued to insist that the dead were buried well outside the city walls but bits and pieces of dead martyrs crept into the city churches as holy relics. The healings that took place more than justified the bending of the rules. This was the first step for the dead to move in among the living. The distinction began to blur between *intra* and *extra mural* [inside and outside the city wall] burials as roadside tombs began to be placed ever closer to the cities. These were the practices among the more wealthy of the European Christians until about the time of the Crusades (A.D. 1096–1291). The poor continued to be buried in nothing more than a winding sheet and laid in common pits outside the city. It will be recalled that in 1791 the impoverished Mozart was buried this same way.[17]

The Crusades were an attempt on the part of Christian Europe to regain the Holy Land, and particularly Jerusalem, from control by the Muslim. The object was to provide safety for the pilgrims and the cause was driven by religious zeal. Nevertheless, throughout the two centuries of virtually continuous conflict lives were lost and the bodies of those Knight Crusaders had to be returned to their families. To have buried them anywhere near Jerusalem would have invited certain mutilation by the incensed Muslim. The common tradesman/soldier who accompanied the Crusaders was often "rendered down" and his bones brought back in a bag, but officers had to be returned intact. Since it was a long and slow journey via Turkey, a gas-tight box was necessary for obvious reasons. The body was enclosed in a container made of lead sheet having soldered joints and this was then supported by a strong outer wooden box. Thus was the heavy sealed coffin made popular among the very wealthy.

In the year A.D. 752 St. Cuthbert of England obtained papal permission to have burial places adjacent to the church building. The churchyard, as it was called, had to be surrounded by a wall and consecrated.[18] It was known as "God's Acre." The purpose of the wall followed from Ezekiel 44:25 and protected the priest from becoming defiled by inadvertently coming near a dead body. Following the Crusades, the wealthy dead began to be buried within the church building even though the church was officially against bringing the dead within a building. The practice was made easier in the case of private churches on the estates of wealthy land owners. In some of these churches the entire sanctuary floor soon consisted of stone casket lids with the family occupants lying beneath. By the Middle Ages every baptized member of the church, was given earth-burial in the sanctified churchyard. When the space was filled the bones were dug up and put in charnel houses leaving space for another body. The system worked leaving church authorities with virtual control over body disposal; the old out of town cemeteries now lay forgotten.

The Laws on body disposal in both Great Britain and North America simply spoke of interment meaning earth burial and there was nothing to prevent anyone using a basket or coffin. The basket coffin was popular in the 1600s but then it became easier and less expensive to produce the closed wooden coffin; this made it more readily available to poorer people. By the early 1800s the simple closed wooden coffin was in extensive use by the common people. However, the closed coffin slowed down the rate of natural decay.[19] After a century or so of burials in the churchyard, the ground surrounding the church had accumulated hundreds of bodies. In some of the larger cities where the rate of disposal far exceeded the rate of decay, the churchyard ground had risen as much as 18 feet above its original level and consisted mostly of decaying remains of coffins and bodies.[20] The smell and the flies were particularly bad on a warm summer day!

The French Revolution

So many of the ills that beset society today were first introduced as ideas, if not in fact, by the shakers and movers of the French Revolution in 1789. The new Republic's prime objective was to supplant the authority of the Roman Church by that of the State, to replace religion by reason, but some of their excesses resulted in the virtual dechristianisation of France. As part of this objective Commissioner of the Convention of the French Directory, Joseph Fouché, issued an order in 1792 to remove all religious emblems from cemeteries and especially to ensure that all burials were conducted without religious ceremony. The burials were to be in a public field in which there was a statue representing Sleep while on the gate of every cemetery was to be a notice proclaiming "Death is eternal sleep." The signs began to appear on cemetery gates in 1794 all over France. It was the word "eternal" that was especially upsetting because for many of the common people in those turbulent times, the only hope left in this life was the assurance of a better life in the next.[21,22] This attack on the belief in the resurrection was the first step to take the psychology of death out of the hands and control of the Church. Less than a century later and with the advance in furnace technology, cremation was introduced in the name of public hygiene. The principal opposition to cremation at that time was the Roman Catholic Church, nevertheless, little by little both Catholic and Protestant Church authority has since been eroded away.

The Garden Cemetery Movement

At the turn of the 1800s there was a humanist reaction to those disease-ridden city churches and with every justification. Proposals were made to build parkland cemeteries outside the cities. This was known as the Garden Cemetery Movement and it had been initiated by the humanist architects of the new Paris following the French Revolution. The significance of the concept was that each cemetery would be run by a public company and have no affiliation with any church. The first Garden Cemetery in America was at Mount Auburn, near Boston, in 1831. In England, the first Garden Cemetery was Kensal Green, opened in 1833, and at that time on the outskirts of London. Kensal Green is now in crumbling decay and entirely surrounded by older houses.

Garden cemeteries were very pleasant and popular places but with the divorce from the sacred they tended to promote the secular. The trend diminished the message of the resurrection and soon emphasized nature worship. Grave markers more often emulated pagan tombs, the cross was seen less and less often and the Christian grave, when present, tended to blend in with the pagan graves beside them. In the late 1800s, the practice of cremation was introduced and, like the scheme to introduce the Garden Cemeteries earlier in that century, began almost simultaneously throughout every country in the Western hemisphere.

While the Garden Cemetery Movement was popular, the Christian community were a tight-knit and conservative lot. They were attached to their own church and familiar place where their ancestors had been buried. City church graveyards continued to become overcrowded, evil-smelling places. Nevertheless, sextons at the church could always be relied upon to find room for one more body. One such sexton was called upon to give evidence before the Edinburgh Magistrates in 1874 and here he explained that the work was usually done at night. The procedure consisted of driving an iron rod—called a "searcher"—into the casket of a previous burial, carefully withdrawing it and, with practiced eye, inspecting the end of the rod to see if its contents were "ripe." If so, the casket and its contents would be exhumed and quietly burned late at night, leaving space for another bereaved but satisfied family.[23] City churches had become centers for disease offering awful smells in the summertime and generally polluting the city drinking water all year round.[24] This was the situation in England, Europe and in the larger cities of North America at the end of the 1800s. Under these conditions it was not too difficult to introduce cremation in the name of public hygiene and safety.

Towards the end of that nineteenth century a few members of the British community recognized that the insanitary conditions had been caused in the first place by the use of closed coffins. Proposals were made to return to earth burial but the authorities were polarized towards their goal of cremation for all. Closed wooden coffins continued and became ever more elaborate, non-destructive and expensive. In North America they were now referred to as caskets. In her 1963 book *The American Way of Death,* Jessica Mitford exposed the ridiculous lengths to which this odious form of public exploitation has been taken.

Rest in Peace

Most readers will probably take it for granted that their remains will stay in the plot without disturbance until the Second Coming. However, history shows that this is unlikely to be the case. For example, in those crowded cities of the world, Athens, Paris and Hong Kong, burial plots are usually rented, not purchased and there is no coffin. The rental time varies from three years in Athens to ten years in Hong Kong and at the end of this period the bones are disinterred, packed neatly in a metal box and returned to the relatives. They may keep them at home or, more usually, the box is sent to an ossuary or mausoleum where they are labeled and stacked and, again, there is a rental charge.

Although there are in Britain and North America strict laws to safeguard cemeteries from say, developers, this does not necessarily mean that human laws are beyond human intervention. The

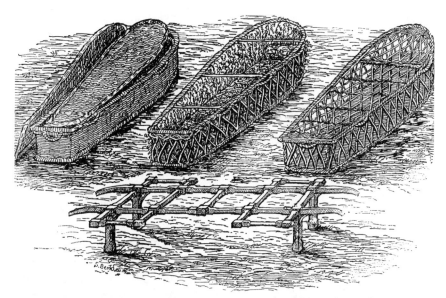

Wicker or basket coffins exhibited in London in 1875. This was part of a sane proposal to maintain the appearance of tradition but ensure that the body return to the earth. Thus, after a few years, would leave room for further interments. The proposal was defeated. [Illustrated London News]

Egyptians buried their dead and took the most elaborate precautions to ensure that the remains of the Pharoahs were secure. The wealthy were buried in cities of the dead that were initially protected by guards. The guards have long gone and visitors to Egypt will be familiar with the famous Tombs of the Memlooks just outside Cairo; in recent years these have become occupied by Cairo's indigent. The common people were buried in pits and became mummified in the dry Egyptian soil. All the care and protection offered to the dead by Egypt in its hey-day meant nothing in the nineteenth century. Those dried cadavers were used to augment the coal-fired steam locomotives of the Egyptian Railway Company while thousands more were "mined," reduced to powder, bagged and sold as fertilizer to English turnip farmers![25] In France following the French Revolution, thousands of bodies were disinterred from Parisien cemeteries to make way for the new boulevards. The bones finished up lining the walls of old underground passageways that are today a macabre tourist attraction.

By now it may be evident to the reader that the dead have not always rested in peace. There were the prayers to the martyrs that eventually led to the rendering down of their bodies for the disposal of parts. An arm bone at this church, and a leg bone at another and so on. Thus, began the cult of relics that flourished throughout the old Latin Church until the thirteenth century. The sainted doctor Thomas Aquinas (1225–1274) is believed to have been murdered but his bones were certainly rendered down and divided among rival monks.[26] The Church had justified this practice by an appeal to the account of returning Joseph's bones from Egypt (Genesis 50:25). However, soon after the Aquinas incident Pope Boniface VIII issued a decretal forbidding the separation of flesh from bones. From this point it was not possible to cut up the dead, and that made it extremely difficult for the proper study of human anatomy. The genius of Michaelangelo permitted him to have special dispensation but not so for the great anatomist Andreas Vesallius (1514–1564) who had to steal a body from a gibbet outside Louvain.

After the Reformation, the Protestant Church continued to forbid the dissection of bodies. In 1726, King George II of England permitted the bodies of all executed criminals to be given to the medical schools for dissection. Up to this point executed murderers were buried although, by tradition, often face downwards and not in God's Acre. Suicides were also excluded from God's Acre. However, even after the Act of 1726 the number of bodies available for the anatomy schools was hopelessly inadequate. Comparative figures are available for the years from 1805 to 1820 during which time there were an average of 75 executions per year. During any one of these years there were over one thousand medical students in London and another thousand in Edinburgh.[27] In consequence, physicians were poorly trained. Medical students in the late 1700s and early 1800s had to exercise a certain amount of ingenuity and not a little courage to obtain a body or even parts for first-hand anatomical study. In post-Revolution Paris, especially about 1792, English, French, and German medical students vied with each other beneath the guillotine to snatch a rolling head or two for study. Stealing from a fresh grave at night was almost a pre-requisite for entrance to the anatomy schools, but then in the 1820s the professionals took over. It may be appreciated that not so very long ago people concerned about their final resting place had good reasons to have placed upon their headstone the words "Rest in Peace."

The Resurrection Men

In England, anatomy schools were beginning to offer handsome sums of money, especially for freaks in good condition. Often they would specify their preference in advance. Sir Astley Cooper, President of the Royal College of Surgeons, had a whole army of grave robbers at his disposal and in 1828 bragged that, "*there is no person ... if I were disposed to dissect, I could not obtain ... The Law only enhances the price, and does not prevent exhumation.*"[28] The eager market of the anatomy schools, ready to pay good prices, attracted full-time operators, who became known as the Resurrection Men.

The two most notorious Resurrection Men were Messrs. Burke and Hare, a couple of Irishmen living in the Edinburgh slums who began their short-lived enterprise in 1827. Their business method was to hasten the departure of their victims with a choke hold or garrote that not only saved a night of exhausting excavation but provided the schools with a fresher body. No questions were asked, while the practice added the expression "burking" to the English language. Burke and Hare were caught, tried and hung in 1829.[29] It was about this time that the practice began of laying a heavy stone on top of the grave; some even had large padlocks and heavy iron bars to prevent theft of the body. The enterprising burial industry offered cast-iron caskets and even fortress-like grave-sites under the name "Mort-safe." Some old Scottish cemeteries still have watchtowers that were built so that the grave of the newly dead could be observed night and day for a week or two to be sure that the body was not stolen or mutilated.[30] The Burke and Hare case precipitated legislation to regulate the British anatomy schools and by 1832 the

Grave installed in 1830 with bronze padlocks and heavy stone cover to prevent theft of the body for the anatomy schools. [Toronto Necropolis. Photo by author.]

Anatomy Act was passed. This allowed private anatomy schools to flourish more openly. However, there still remained the problem not only of obtaining good cadavers but keeping them long enough to be useful for anatomy classes. Eventually, the problem was largely overcome by patented embalming techniques that were developed during the American Civil War of 1861–1865. The practice of embalming thus made year-round teaching of anatomy possible, put a final end to the body snatching business and established embalming as a tradition today.[31]

Modern western jurisprudence in based upon two legal systems: Jewish and the Roman usually now referred to as Ecclesiastical and Common Law. Until the French Revolution the wielders of Ecclesiastical Law, whether Catholic or Protestant, had far greater power than they do today. The matter of disposal of the dead came under Ecclesiastical jurisdiction but there were really no laws to protect the dead body. From time to time there would be a disturbing case where a Roman monk sought to punish a Protestant heretic as happened to Wycliffe. Then again, some practioner of diabolism might be caught taking parts for his black arts, but disturbing the dead was generally not a problem. The authorities tended to look the other way when, say, cases were brought to their attention of those caught extracting the teeth from cadavers and selling them to the local dentist. Some even rendered down bodies to make candles; dead children were said to make the best candles.[32] Thus it was that prior to 1788 English Law argued that there was no property in a dead body and that theft of a body was stealing "*nothing from nobody*" and not a punishable offence. Curiously however, if the shroud or any grave articles were included with the body then the thief was charged with theft of these items. Following the Anatomy Act of 1832, the law was modified, at first to make grave robbery punishable as a misdemeanour and finally a Bill was passed to prevent unlawful disinterment of human bodies.

In the next chapter the story continues in Victorian England. In the opening sentence to his *Tale of Two Cities*, Charles Dickens said of London and Paris in the 1780s: "*it was the best of times, it was the worst of times.*" After the Revolution, Paris changed but London continued in opulence, poverty and hypocrisy for another century. This was the century that produced Charles Darwin and Karl Marx, introduced spiritualism and a dozen new Churches—most of them Christian in name only—and throughout, the shadowy hand of freemasonry can just be discerned.

2

The Continuing Conspiracy

And if there be no meeting past the grave,
If all is darkness, silence, yet 'tis rest.
For God still giveth his beloved sleep,
And if an endless sleep he wills, so best.

AN AGNOSTIC'S TOMB EPIGRAPH — T. H. HUXLEY

The Nineteenth Century Campaign

In the mid-1800s, the cities of Great Britain and Europe, and particularly their church cemeteries, had become centers of disease. This provided exactly the kind of justification to introduce cremation to a general public that at that time had a fairly strong Christian ethic. Not only among Christians but also the general public, the burning of the dead was associated with a kind of posthumous punishment reserved for murderers and heretics. It was the medical profession who led the way to reverse this thinking and did so in the interests of public health. The first bold steps were taken at the Medical International Congress held in Florence, Italy, in 1869. Cremation Societies were formed in several of the principal cities in Europe and the first crematorium was built in Dresden, Germany, and began operation in 1874. The following year the industrialist, Albert Keller, built a public crematorium in Milan, Catholic Italy. In the rest of Europe, and particularly in Britain, there was some opposition from the clergy and Sir Henry Thompson, who had been an active promoter at the Medical Congress in Florence, now began a program of persuasion by scholarly words in stuffy Victorian periodicals.

Sir Henry Thompson (1820–1904), urogenital physician to many crowned heads of Europe and surgeon to Queen Victoria, had quietly laid the ground work with his lengthy paper published in the January 1874 issue of *The Contemporary Review*.[1] In this paper he had set out every possible argument why cremation should be adopted and he had met every possible objection. The paper sparked lively debate among the *literi*, but it took Dr. Price's hilltop

15

Sir John Everett Millais
1829–1896

Sir Thomas Spencer Wells
1818–1897

Shirley Brooks
1816–1874

Sir Henry Thompson
1820–1904

Sir John Tenniel
1820–1914

Frederick A. Lehmann
1826–1891
His bride: Nina Chambers

Anthony Trollope
1818–1882

The founding members of England's Cremation Society
[Illustrated London News & Metro Toronto Reference Library]

outrage in 1893 to really bring the issue to public attention. However, Sir Henry Thompson and his little band of seven like-minded individuals, several of whom are known to have been freemasons, had formed the Cremation Society in 1874 to promote the practice by less dramatic means.[2] At that time, cremation was not yet legal in Britain, and steady pressure had to be applied to the legal profession and especially to the clergy by published papers.[3-5]

The Cremation Society in Britain still operates today and is integrated with twenty-six similar organizations around the world as the International Cremation Federation. In England, it is the Cremation Society that, since its inception, has been the driving force to promote cremation by pamphlets and posters principally through the Church of England. Whenever possible an Anglican Bishop's good words of approval are sought and given the widest possible circulation. A sampling of published quotes from Bishops of the Church of England advocating cremation will be found in Appendix A. From these episcopal words the reader will gain some insight into the actual belief in the Word of God held to by these gentlemen.

Another successful means of promoting cremation was and still is to publish the names of the famous who had requested this form of disposal. For example, at the Golders Green crematorium in London, England, every repository of a well-known name is clearly marked for the benefit of the visitor. A sample of some of the names of England's famous will quickly alert the reader to the fact that without exception all were humanists: Somerset Maugham; Ernest Bevin; T. S. Eliot; Havelock Ellis; Friedrich Engels; Julian Huxley; Rudyard Kipling; Tom Mann; Harry Pollitt; George Bernard Shaw; Marie Stopes; and H. G. Wells to name a few. The otherwise uninformed visitor concerned with a personal question about cremation is likely to come away from the quite beautiful gardens of Golders Green thinking, if cremation was good enough for these famous people, it must surely be good enough for me. As time passed more Bishops of the Church of England became supporters of the Cremation Movement and when their turn came they chose to support "the better way." Archbishop William Temple, known as The Red Dean, was the first cremated primate of England and given much publicity at his departure in 1944; Archbishop Lord Lang followed him to the furnace in 1946. In February of 2002 Princess Margaret took the first bold step for British royalty since the pagan Viking kings of pre-Christian Britain.

LA CRÉMATION ET SES PROCÉDÉS : LE FOUR A CRÉMATION DE L'APPAREIL GARINI EMPLOYÉ A MILAN (Voir l'article, page 274).

The first crematorium to open in Milan, Catholic Italy, in 1876. The illustration shows no indication of a forced draught for the furnace thus, the operation would have been very inefficient. [National Library of Canada]

The Freemasonry Connection

The methods of promoting cremation, an idea repugnant to many of the public, must be subtle, seemingly have every practical justification and even be given the Church's blessing. All this has happened yet, as we shall see later, not all of it can be ascribed to human conspiracy. Following the Medical International Congress of 1869, promotion was active and organized while opposition from the clergy was at first strong but then gradually diminished. Most of the forceful objections had been that cremation would destroy the belief in the resurrection and many writers in the Roman Church expressed these thoughts best. Some of the following quotations, referenced to Irion (1968) in this section, have actually been taken from the primary source, Father David Dorsett. Dorsett managed to have his work published in a Cremation Society journal and this is the primary reference, however, Irion's book is likely to be more readily available to the reader. Regarding the resistance to the introduction of cremation in revolutionary France, Irion paraphrased Dorsett as follows:

> *"It is important to note that the official opposition of the Roman Catho-lic Church was not based on theological grounds, for cremation has never been held to be in conflict with the dogma of that church ... The Roman Catholic church ... saw a threat* [to Church authority] *as many leaders of cremation societies were freemasons or agnostics."*[6]

A second Catholic source having these same sentiments is more blunt and asserts that, *"the attempt to introduce the practice* [cremation] *into Christian society was un-Christian and Masonic in motivation."*[7] It is insightful to see what a representative of the Masonic organization says in a direct reply to Dorsett:

> *"The Freemason, Ghisleri, in his Almanacco dei liberi muratori writes: 'Catholics have good reason to oppose cremation. The purification of death by fire will shake to its foundations Catholic predominance on the terror with which it has surrounded death.'"*[8]

When cremation was introduced into Milan, Italy, in 1875, there was no official pronouncement against the practice until Pope Leo XIII issued a series of edicts in 1886. Then Canon laws 1203 and 1240 forbade Roman Catholics to have any thing to do with crema-tion. However, in 1963 the Roman Church gave in and now per-mits cremation with its blessing. Many readers will understand that freemasonry and the Roman Church are diametrically opposed but it should also be understood that, like nations that pose a threat to each other, each side has "moles"or spies in the opposite camp. Giovanni Mastai-Ferretti (1792–1878) was a member of the Masonic order until he became Pope Pius IX then left the order well informed and promptly declared ex-communication on all freemasons within the Catholic Church.[9] The bottom line is that the Roman church is and always has been, extremely well informed about its opposition.

When the new crematorium was opened in Milan, Italy, in 1876, it had been the work of the Cremation Society, a dedicated band of freemasons with an anti-Christian campaign. In the British Museum there is a pamphlet written by a member of that Society, professor Gorini, and published in Milan in 1876 some months after the cre-matorium had been in operation. In his pamphlet he makes the fol-lowing statement:

> *"Our task is not confined to the mere burning of the dead, but extends to burning and destroying superstition as well."* Professor Gorini then

advocated selling the ashes of the dead to farmers saying: "*The result would be that this common material would partially return to be re-incarnated in the bodies of the living Milanese. This is the only resurrection of the body recognized by science.*"[10]

The freemason's view of the afterlife may be found in the *Encyclopedia of Freemasonry* under "Resurrection." After almost a full column in which the beliefs of the resurrection from the Egyptian, Babylonian and finally the Christian view are mentioned, the Masonic position is finally given in the following statement:

"*Our Order is a positive contradiction to Judaic blindness and infidelity, and testifies our faith concerning the resurrection of the body.*"[11]

Masonic texts are fond of the word "arcane" meaning known or knowable only to the initiate and this statement is a classic case based upon ambiguity. In the first place, the majority of Jews in the past have always believed in the resurrection; only the minority were influenced by Greek philosophy, or today by intellectualism and do not believe. Secondly, no one should believe in the "resurrection of the body." Scripture consistently speaks of "resurrection of the dead" and this is the foundation for Jewish and Christian belief. The Masonic text could have been written simply: "Our Order believes in the resurrection of the dead." As it stands, however, it can be read in two opposite ways, that is, read by the uninitiated [the profane] as upholding the belief in the resurrection and read by senior initiates [the adepts] as rejecting that belief. The Masonic rite of Hiram Abif is a pagan rebirth ritual and counterfeit of the Christian rebirth and baptism; it has nothing whatsoever to do with resurrection after physical death. The Masonic burial rites with the acacia branch, etc. speak of "resurrection of the body," but their real meaning, as those who graduate to the higher degrees discover, is that the mason "lives on through his progeny." Thus, the true Masonic understanding is that death is followed by oblivion and, as Professor Gorini implied, the Christian doctrine of the general resurrection is regarded as pure superstition.

In their concern for the promotion of cremation by the Cremation Society in Milan, the Holy Office of the Roman Catholic church issued their formal statement in Latin by their official publication *Codis juris canonici fontes*. Article 1100 for May 19, 1886. It states in part and in translation:

"Not a few bishops and sincere members of the faithful, being aware that men of uncertain faith or pledged to the Masonic sect are striving today with great effort that the pagan custom of burning human corpses be introduced ..."[12]

In response to this Article, the president of the Cremation Society, Dr. Malachia, and the secretary, Dr. Pini, published a pamphlet defending cremation and everyone affiliated with the Cremation Societies. The French writer, A. Faucieux, writing from the Roman Catholic position for the *Revue des Sciences Ecclésiastiques,* provides a full quote from this rather informative Masonic pamphlet issued by lodge M to the brethren. Here the objectives of freemasonry in promoting cremation are clearly spelled out. In translation it reads as follows:

"The Roman Church, this implacable enemy of the human race, ... brings us a challenge in condemnation of cremating bodies that our society has until now spread with most beautiful results ... The FF [Lodge Brothers] therefore should employ all methods to spread the use of cremation and make it universal. Our purpose is to establish in the cities and country committees charged with propagating cremation and making known by word and pen that the greatest honors will be rendered to those who in death will give up their bodies to the Cremation Society. Finally, recalling throughout that if the priests are horrified at cremation, it is because in all things, he is partisan with ignorance and he is looking with speculation on the dead to reap a vile reward ... The Church, in forbidding the burning of bodies, is asserting her rights over the living and the dead; over the consciences of men as well as over their bodies, and is merely seeking to preserve among people the old beliefs in the immortality of the soul and in a future life—beliefs overthrown today by the light of science .... The Lodge M has confidence in your caution and your wisdom ... Receive our fraternal greeting." [13]

In his conclusion to his article containing this long quote by the lodge, Faucieux writes: *"The declaration is clear: The great inspirer of this new war against religion and the church, is freemasonry. She gives as a pretext, science and humanity."* [14]

One may question if the effect of the promotional campaign and subsequent establishment of the practice of cremation within the Christian community has been the cause of disbelief in the future resurrection. This is one of those cause and effect equations that are often difficult to prove. Nevertheless, as an indication anyone can inspect Dodd's Peerage at the local reference library and see for themselves the names and initiation dates into the Masonic brotherhood of many, though not all, of the bishops of the Church of England. Then we observe the high profile bishops in the Church of England who have publically declared their unbelief in the resurrection and have survived in their position. It is the survival that tells the bigger story.

In 1963, the highly controversial book *Honest to God* by Bishop John T. Robinson questioned the Virgin Birth and the Resurrection of Christ, two of the most basic doctrines of Christianity. He survived.[15] At Christmas time, 1983, senior Anglican churchman, David Jenkins appeared as guest on the British national television program, *Credo*. During this program he was asked about the Virgin Birth and the Resurrection and his answers gave the distinct impression that he did not believe in either of them. He later denied this but the fact remains that 20,000 viewers understood what he had said and sent in a petition to Archbishop Runcie to have Jenkins removed from his position. Runcie rejected the petition. David Jenkins not only survived but a few months later, in July 1984, was consecrated as Bishop of Durham in Yorkminster Cathedral.[16] Interestingly, lightning struck and burned down the south transcept of the Cathedral a few days later.[17]

We may write these occurences off as coincidental but not the fire insurance company who declared it to be an act of God and refused to pay! For those interested in these coincidences a similar fire destroyed the Universal studios in Hollywood in November of 1990. It was this studio that had been responsible for distributing the blasphemous film *The Last Temptation of Christ*. So, we may ask, does the average churchgoer believe in the resurrection? In a British national survey conducted by the MORI Institute in 1994 it was found that ten per cent of churchgoers do not believe in the Resurrection of Christ. If there is this much disbelief in the resurrection of their Founder, we can only imagine how much skepticism there is in the promised resurrection of the individual Christian? The doctrine of the resurrection is also under attack from another direction. The Second Coming of Christ has been openly questioned and, according to Scripture, this event immediately precedes the resurrection:

2 Peter 3:3-4

> Knowing this first: that scoffers will come in the last days,
> walking according to their own lusts and saying,
> "Where is the promise of His coming? ..."

From this chapter, we may appreciate how step by step, body disposal practices among the Christian West, both Catholic and Protestant elements, have departed from the original commandment to return to the dust. We have instead adopted non-burial practices that have brought health hazards to the cities and justified the introduction of cremation. Cremation is possibly the most blatant form of disobedience and, as we shall see later, this is compounded when the ashes are scattered. We shall further see that continued disobedience has serious consequences for the living. However, it does need to be made clear here that Christians will be judged by the spirit of the law rather than by the letter. In other words, it is our heart attitude towards the Scriptures that is most important. For example, if we put the authority of Scripture first and choose to return to the earth but say, unfortunately die in a house fire, then we have not been disobedient to the spirit of the Law. On the other hand, if we consciously choose to disobey the Scripture and listen to all the usual humanistic arguments for cremation, then this is plainly disobedient to both the letter and the spirit of the law.

A final word concerns the financial motivation that promotes cremation. Public cemeteries are often in private hands. For a given investment calculated initially on say, 1200 burials per acre, the return on this investment can be greatly improved by increasing that number. This has long been done by vertical placement: downwards by stacking four or five coffins in a single plot and upwards by mausoleum towers. However, cremation offers an even greater potential for economy of space. All told, cemetery real estate is regarded by the financial industry as a rather sound investment.[18] As far as the individual is concerned, cremation is indeed currently less expensive but only relatively so compared to the exhorbitant cost of burial. We might be reminded that it was the unscriptural use of box burial in the first place that caused the costs to rise and introduced the justification for cremation. The relatively lower cost of cremation is a means of self promotion but we can be sure that once the practice is made mandatory costs will quickly rise to meet or even exceed those of burial. As it is, crematoria already insist upon the use of a non-reusable casket to handle the body.

— o◯o —

3

Attacking the Resurrection

And if Christ is not risen, your faith is futile; you are
still in your sins! Then also those who have fallen asleep
in Christ have perished. If in this life only we have hope
in Christ, we are of all men most pitiable.

PAUL OF TARSUS, C. A.D. 56

What do We Mean by the Resurrection?

It is always a good idea to define our terms. In the following chapters
we are not referring to the Resurrection of Christ, usually written
with a capital "R," but rather the general resurrection of humanity,
written with a small "r." The writers Matthew and Luke had chosen
their words carefully when referring to the resurrection of humanity
and had consistently spoken of the "resurrection of the dead [*nek-*
ros]." Whereas when Paul used his analogy of the planted seed (1
Cor. 15:37ff), he correctly used the word "body" [*soma*]. The word
soma used alone normally means a "living body" which precisely describes the seed. If Paul had meant dead body he would have used
the word *ptoma*. The Gospel writers had simply said "dead" not "dead
body"so that they are not necessarily referring to the physical body.
To retain the consistency expected of Scripture they are referring to
the person, the soul. The Apostles' Creed has been the cause of
some confusion in this respect. Further, the passage in Romans 8:11
is not in the context of the resurrection and speaks of "mortal bodies" not "glorified bodies." It has to be admitted that the thought of a
dead and rotting body or simply the dust coming to life again is difficult for the Christian to visualize and impossible for the materialist
to accept. Yet, this is Christianity's principal doctrine and has been
fervently held to by millions. It sometimes helps by first accepting
that God created Adam from the pristine dust of the ground; each
new atom brought precisely to its assigned place. In the case of the
resurrection of the dead, the analogy of the seed is a good one and
indicates that the resurrection process is not confined to using the

same atoms as in the original body anymore than the same atoms are used that were in the original plant.

Widespread Belief in the Resurrection

The belief in the resurrection of the dead is one of mankind's most ancient beliefs. One of the earliest civilizations, the Egyptians, were totally dedicated to the idea and went to enormous and well-known lengths to keep the body in good shape for the expected future event.[1] Of course, only the very wealthy could afford all the elaborate preparation and means of subsequent protection. The pyramids were only a means to this end and played no part in protection. Many other nations, from the aborigines of Australia to the Zoroastrians of Persia, from northern Canada to Patagonia all believed in a future resurrection and commonly buried their dead in a sitting position.[2-5] The Indians explained that in this way they would be better placed when they rise on the last day. It was common for those Indian nations of North and South Americas to bury the body facing West so that they could return to the land of their ancestors suggesting that they came from across the Pacific. Early Christians of Europe generally buried in the supine [sleeping] position with the head towards the East. The belief in the resurrection of the dead was a surprise to missionaries and has baffled the evolutionary mind-set of the anthropologists. Firstly, the discovery that tribes from one end of the earth to the other had a common belief in the resurrection suggested one geographical origin for mankind; perhaps there was some truth to the dispersal from the Tower of Babel? Secondly, the very idea of the resurrection of the dead is really quite fantastic and makes it difficult to deny that early man must have been sufficiently sophisticated to have thought of it in the first place. The evolutionary image of multiple origins of the cave-man just does not fit these facts.

A mummy of the Muysca Indian buried in the sitting position. Throughout North and South America the Indians explained to the missionaries that buried in this position they would be ready for the resurrection. [Fisher Rare Book Library, Toronto.]

The Pagan Background

Prior to the time of Christ there had long been a difference of opinion among the peoples of the eastern Mediterranean countries regarding the destiny of the soul. In the very distant past the Orientals, notably in India and Persia, considered existence a curse rather than a blessing and for them nirvana, or the annihilation of the soul, was their ultimate hope. For others, a more attractive prospect was that of eternal existence. However, since it was evident that the body decayed at death, the soul was said to be a separate entity trapped within a living body during life but released upon death. In this philosophic view souls were separable from the body at death and even at times during life through the influence of drugs; the doctrine is called dualism. In this doctrine souls were immortal but restricted without the material body. The doctrine of reincarnation, or metempsychosis to give it a more obscure name, then developed whereby souls were passed on from body to body gradually working their way towards perfection. These Oriental views were picked up by the Greeks via Egypt and given their classical formulation in the dialogues of Plato four centuries before Christ.

Plato (c.428–348) had evidently been influenced by the account of a young Greek soldier named Er who had been killed on the battlefield then, during cremation of the bodies, he came back to life and related his experience while out of his body. The account may be found in the very last chapter of Plato's book *The Republic.*[6] That chapter is titled *The Immortality of the Soul* and the topic runs throughout Plato's writings. Plato introduced the immortal soul of man in his creation account given in his *Timaeus*[7] (lines 41, 43, 69). In his *Phaedrus*[8] Plato's view of the soul was that because it was self-moving it was unbegotten, immortal and indestructible (245) while in his *Laws*[9] he maintained that the soul has at least two parts, one part good and another evil (10:896). However, it is in his *Phaedo*[10] that he went into greatest detail. He recounted the last conversation with his master, Socrates, who was about to take the fatal dose of hemlock. Socrates had convinced everyone of his visitors that death was merely the separation of the soul from the body (64) while the soul was the seeker of eternal truth and thus itself immortal. He argued that the body's senses are notoriously untrustworthy and mislead the soul in her search for the truth (65). Death then meant freedom for the conscious soul and Socrates was joyfully looking forward to this experience. Plato expanded on this theme saying that the human soul was immortal like the gods (80) and, whatever pain it might endure, the soul could not cease to be (106). He

Socrates (470–399 B.C.) in prison telling his students his theories of the soul. Plato was absent. He willingly accepted the cup of hemlock being offered and looked forward to being set free from the body. Engraving after the painting done in 1787 by Jacques-Louis David. [Metro Toronto Reference Library]

added that impure souls would pass into the bodies of asses and wolves (82) and that there would be judgment and punishment (113). His evidence for immortality was based upon what he perceived as inherent knowledge and cited those déjà vu moments that most of us have experienced when we sense that we have been here before (73–76). He believed that our soul had existed in a previous life. There is, in fact, a perfectly good physiological explanation for those déjà vu experiences. When there is a momentary retardation of the nerve signal in one eye or one ear this causes the brain to receive the same signal twice but just micro-seconds apart. Thus, Plato was teaching the Oriental ideas of dualism [soul separation], the immortality of the soul, judgment, retribution and reincarnation.

Aristotle, Plato's most illustrious student, at one time supported Plato's immortal soul but finally he argued against it. There were other Greek philosophers in that heady intellectual circle that was Athens who, as pragmatists, saw in a dead body finality with no evidence whatsoever of existence after death. Least of all could any of these views accept the preposterous notion of those strange Jews who spoke of a resurrection of the dead. The resurrection was a belief that had been steadfastly held to in that intellectual Greek community only by a handful of Jews. In spite of these opposing views, Plato's teaching outlasted all others, influenced the early Church and remains in the Church to this day. One reason that Plato's teachings have had such a great influence on the Western Church is that the Academy he founded was in continued existence for over nine hundred years (387 B.C. – A.D. 529). This record is unmatched by any other academic institution, before or since. A second reason is that Plato's works were first translated into Latin by Fincino in 1484. Since that time the English literary establishment from Edmund Spencer to Coleridge, Shelley, and especially Wordsworth and William Blake all became neo-platonists and promoted the idea of the immortal and separable soul by words and illustration.

The Pagan Influence Upon Christianity

Most of the Jews, as keepers of God's revealed truth to mankind, steadfastly held to the belief in the resurrection and based their doctrine upon the Scriptures and the Mosaic oral tradition. Job chapter 14 and Daniel 12:2 were the key passages for their belief:

Job 14:14

> If a man dies, shall he live again? All the days of my hard
> service I will wait. Till my change comes. You shall call,
> and I will answer You;

Daniel 12:2

> And many of those who sleep in the dust of the earth
> shall awake, some to everlasting life, some to shame
> and everlasting contempt.

In the Greek colony of Alexandria, northern Egypt, lived a large number of Jews. Some of their scribes were responsible for translating the Hebrew Old Testament into the Greek version known as the Septuagint. Just at the time of Christ, a Jewish philosopher named Philo (13 B.C. – A.D. 45) who, well steeped in the teaching of Plato— he was known as the Jewish Plato—began to influence this Jewish colony. Philo caused many of these Greek-speaking Jews to abandon their faith in the resurrection. The timing of the first Advent was thus crucial to the survival of this belief among the Chosen People.

Many readers will recall that the Sadducees did not believe in the resurrection either but their reasoning was not caused by Greek

Etching done in 1808 by William Blake to illustrate Robert Blair's poem "The Grave."
Blake was a neo-platonist and his illustrations greatly influenced Victorian readers.
In Hebrew the soul is in the feminine gender. [Metro Toronto Reference Library]

philosophy. The Sadducees were very conservative followers of the
priest Zadok, rejected Mosaic oral tradition and stuck strictly to the
written word, mostly the Pentateuch. The Alexandrian Jews on the
other hand, had been persuaded to adopt Plato's separable and immortal soul. Some of their writings have survived and may be found
in the inter-testamental apochrypha e.g. *The Wisdom of Solomon* 3:4
and 15:3 written about 50 B.C. At the time of Paul and the apostles,
the destiny of the soul was the hot question of all questions among
the various schools of Greek philosophy none of which included a
resurrection. Thus, when Paul brought the resurrection message to
the materialist Greeks in Corinth, most of his audience regarded
the idea as pure foolishness:

1 Corinthians 1:23
> But we preach Christ crucified, to the Jews a stumbling
> block and to the Greeks foolishness.

Paul would have been fully knowledgeable of the teachings of the
Greek philosophers and their endless debates about the afterlife.
He would certainly have been conversant with the teachings of Plato

and his transmigration or reincarnation of immortal souls. It is likely then that he had this in mind when writing his letter to the Romans.

Romans 5:14-21

> Nevertheless death reigned from Adam to Moses,... For if by the one man's [Adam] offense many died, ... For if by the one man's offense death reigned through the one, ... Therefore, as through one man's offense judgment came to all ... For as by one man's disobedience many were made sinners, ...

Here Paul makes it absolutely clear by repetition that sin was introduced by one man, the man Adam, and not from a previous existence of the individual. Scripture nowhere speaks of a mysterious previous existence or previous race. The teaching of a pre-adamite race sometimes heard among Christians arose out of a racist attempt by European Christians in the fifteenth century to explain the origin of the colored peoples but it is not supported by Scripture.[11]

The first Christians were taught by the apostles but within a generation or so Plato's ideas began to creep in. First by Church Father Athanogoras about A.D. 187, amplified by Tertullian a few years later then thoroughly established by the sainted Augustine (A.D. 354–430) in his *City of God*. Augustine had given his stamp of approval to Plato speaking of him in the most glowing terms: "*Plato is the one who shone with the glory which far excelled that of all others*" and "*To Plato is given the praise of having perfected philosophy ...*"[12] Augustine also gave praise to the platonists, those graduates of Plato's Academy that was still a revered institution in Augustine's day and was not closed until a century after his death. Naturally, Augustine accepted Plato's immortal soul,[13] however, he did reject Plato's ideas on reincarnation. The Christian twist on Plato's teaching is referred to today as new or neoplatonism.

A little earlier, another Church Father, Origen (A.D. 185–254), adopted a new method of interpretation based upon allegory. In this, he was able to depart from the literal meaning of Scripture, adopt Plato's teaching on the soul and allegorize those Scriptures that described the fate of the wicked. He disliked the idea of the wicked suffering for all eternity and taught instead that all the wicked and unbelievers would eventually be restored and given eternal life in heaven. He was finally condemned as a heretic for this teaching by the other Church Fathers but the notion still lingers on

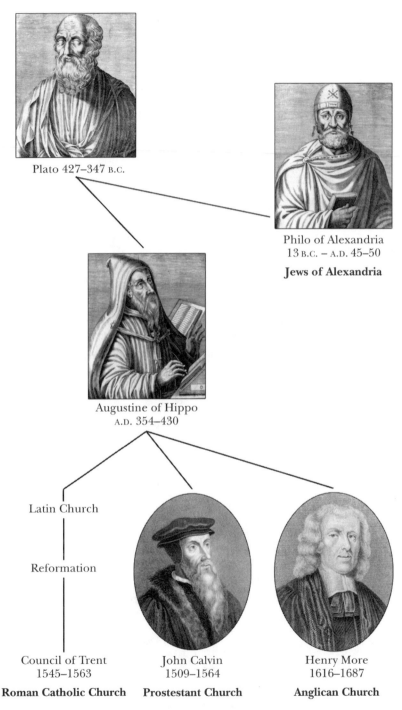

Plato 427–347 B.C.

Philo of Alexandria
13 B.C. – A.D. 45–50
Jews of Alexandria

Augustine of Hippo
A.D. 354–430

Latin Church

Reformation

Council of Trent
1545–1563
Roman Catholic Church

John Calvin
1509–1564
Prostestant Church

Henry More
1616–1687
Anglican Church

How the idea of the immortal soul traveled from the Greeks to the Church.

today among the cults. It is known as Universalism, and teaches that all roads lead to heaven.

In spite of Origen and Augustine's followers, many of the ante-Nicean and post-Nicean Church Fathers remained faithful to the early teaching of the Church. Nevertheless, throughout the centuries neo-platonism was increasingly adopted by the Church leaders principally through the writings of Augustine. Finally, in the Fifth Lateran Council (1512–1517), innate immortality of the soul was declared to be a Church dogma. The word "innate" was prefixed to "immortality" and means "immortal from birth" and not from eternity past.

It was at about this time, the early 1500s, that a growing number of European Christians, totally disenchanted by the wealthy, powerful institution that the old Latin/Roman Catholic Church had become, called for a renewed church. Part of this disenchanted number were some who were given the name "Anabaptists." While they did not welcome this name, they were given it because they were perceived to have been re-baptized, that is, the first time sprinkled as a babe and the second time immersed as an adult. The Anabaptists sought to separate the Church from government and restore it to its original simplicity; they also rejected neo-platonism. They were absolutely sincere in their beliefs but were viewed as extremists by both Catholics and later by Protestants. While this may have been tolerable, their rejection of Plato and the traditional teaching of salvation through infant baptism [christening] was regarded as a dangerous heresy that undermined the authority of the Church. By 1527 a campaign of active persecution by the Roman Church began against the Anabaptists; many were burned at the stake.

Then the followers of John Calvin (1509–1564), who still regarded themselves as Catholics but were in effect the pre-natal Protestant Church, added their voice to the general persecution. Calvin wrote in 1534 of that, "*nefarious herd of Anabaptists ... nothing could be more absurd than this* [soul sleep], *O pernicious pest! O tares certainly sown by an enemy's hand ...*" Calvin opposed them because they did not accept neo-platonism.[14] The Anabaptist were virtually exterminated until only a handful remained who then became known by their leader's names as the Hussites and the Mennonites. In seventeenth century England, Plato's teaching on the immortal soul was given fresh impetus by the Cambridge neo-platonists led by Benjamin Whichcote (1609–1683) and the writings of Henry More.[15] The Cambridge neo-platonists were

Anabaptist, Anne Hendriks was burned to death for her faith in 1571 in Amsterdam by Catholics loyal to Spain. She was tied to a ladder and her mouth filled with a bag of gunpowder to prevent her from "making a good witness." The ladder was pushed onto a bed of burning coals. [*Mirror of the Martyrs* by John S. Oyer reproduced by Good Books, PA]

also responsible for introducing the Greek ideas of evolution into the Church. However, their promotion of the soul's immortality was so successful that the subject "neo-platonism" will rarely be found in modern evangelical Christian text books today. Like the Roman Church before them, the North American Protestant Church doctrine on the soul now has the authority of unquestioned tradition. Once again, we should be reminded that this popular belief that the human soul is immortal originated from the lying promise given to Eve:

Genesis 2:17
> God to Adam: "… tree of the knowledge … you shall not eat, for in the day that you eat of it you shall surely die,"

Genesis 3:4
> Satan lied to Eve: "You will not surely die …"

Genesis 3:22

> Adam and Eve were expelled from the Garden:
> "… lest he put out his hand and take also of the tree of life, and eat, and live forever —"

Adam and Eve did not eat of the tree of life, thus, would not live forever, therefore were not immortal and, consequently, it is difficult to explain how their descendants can be immortal. The following sections document some of the attempts made to undermine the belief in the resurrection. It should be borne in mind that if we are indeed innately immortal then our conscious soul must separate from the dead body and, if Protestant, go either directly to heaven or to hell. Either way, and whether we are saint or sinner, this puts into question the need for the resurrection of the dead, the glorified body and the judgment.

The Resurrection Is Already Past

The gospel of Matthew was written between A.D. 58–68 and three intriguing little verses tell us all too cryptically of a miraculous event that occurred after the Resurrection of Christ:

Matthew 28:51-53

> … and the graves were opened and the bodies of the saints who had fallen asleep were raised; and coming out of the graves after His resurrection, they went into the holy city and appeared to many.

This account comes right in the middle of the account of Christ's crucifixion and the reader would naturally conclude that the event occurred at the time of the crucifixion. Verse 53 tells us that it occurred **after** the Resurrection. It may have been days or even years later we are not told, and neither are we told that they had glorified bodies but simply that they *"appeared to many."* As we shall see below in the case of the Seven Sleepers of Ephesus, this miracle was probably intended to reinforce the promise of the general resurrection. Nevertheless, the event was likely responsible for the rumor that the general resurrection had already taken place.

In his second letter to Timothy written in A.D. 67, up to nine years after Matthew's gospel, Paul warns about a heresy being spread and named two characters responsible for spreading it:

2 Timothy 2:16-18

> But shun profane and vain babblings, for they will increase
> to more ungodliness. And their message will spread like a
> cancer. Hymenaeus and Philetus are of this sort, who have
> strayed concerning the truth saying that the resurrection is
> already past; and they overthrow the faith of some.

Paul was probably concerned about those who had heard this account that had the authority of Matthew as its author but had been
used to claim that the general resurrection had already taken place.
Thus, all hope for their own resurrection was destroyed. In the
memory of those who, thirty years earlier, had witnessed the raising
of those Old Testament saints, the effectiveness of this type of deception would have been far greater than, say, it would be today.

The Seven Sleepers of Ephesus

The attack on the resurrection in this case was the forced renuncia-
tion of Christ by the Roman authorities. Renouncing Christ also
renounced the resurrection to eternal life. One of the most wide-
spread of Christian legends concerns the Roman emperor Decius
who came to Ephesus about the year A.D. 250 and demanded that all
should sacrifice to idols. Most Christians refused including seven
young men who eventually took refuge in a cave. They were discovered and the cave walled in with large stones. About 140 years later,
at a time when the doctrine of the resurrection was being challenged, a farmer needed the stones and the youths were discovered
alive. They explained to the startled populace that God had raised
them up before the Resurrection Day to be witnesses to the fact that
they had been sleeping. After that the seven laid their heads on the
ground and gave back their spirits according to the will of God.

Matthew's account [28:51-53] given above is very likely of a similar
kind and is a Scriptural precedent for the account of the Seven
Sleepers. The purpose of both accounts would seemingly be to
counter the denial of the general resurrection and to be witness to
the fact that they had been sleeping and not in heaven or in hell.
The story of the Seven Sleepers of Ephesus is recounted several
times throughout Church history, is in many ancient documents,
Jewish and Moslem, and suggests that it had a single, factual origin.[16]

In summary, we have seen how the lie in the Garden of Eden was
introduced to Western cultures from the East by doctrines of reincarnation and the duality of the soul. This was picked up and greatly
expanded by the Greek philosopher, Plato, who claimed the soul to

be immortal. Plato's views on the soul were taught for almost nine centuries throughout the Greek and Roman empires. These ideas were introduced to the Alexandrian Jews by Philo just before the ministry of Christ and caused them to lose their belief in the resurrection. The teaching of the New Testament re-established the doctrine of the resurrection but again, Plato's message was introduced to the Church principally through the writings of Augustine. The old Latin Church and Roman Catholic Church doctrine on the destiny of the soul is based upon Augustine's writings. With his Latin/Catholic background John Calvin carried Augustine's neo-platonic interpretation of the soul into the early Protestant Church. From about this same time, the Christian Church began to depart from the Scriptural injuction to return the dead to the earth. This led to a public health situation that justified the introduction of cremation. Cremation is a powerful means of sustaining the belief in the immortal and separable soul and cause a loss of faith in the general resurrection. We shall see in the next chapter some of the more subtle means by which the neo-platonic teaching on the immortal soul has been sustained in the Christian Church for at least eighteen centuries.

4

Some of the More Subtle Methods

Sleep; and if life was bitter to thee, pardon,
If sweet, give thanks; thou hast no more to live;
And to give thanks is good, and to forgive.

A.C. SWINBURNE. *AVE ATQUE VALE.* 1878

The Apostles' Creed

Very early in Church history it was felt necessary to have a statement of belief that could be rehearsed at the water baptism of the new converts. Scholars generally agree that this took place near the end of the second century and produced what is called today The Old Roman Creed. It is not thought to be the work of the apostles themselves and comes in a number of variant forms. It is the oldest creed and the one to which every Christian Church, both East and West, can agree. With later additions, this Creed became the familiar Apostles' Creed:

I believe in God almighty [or Father almighty]
And in Jesus Christ His only Son, our Lord
Who was born of the Holy Spirit and the Virgin Mary
Who was crucified under Pontius Pilate and was buried
[A later addition: He descended into hell]
And the third day rose from the dead
Who ascended into heaven
And sits on the right hand of the Father
Whence He comes to judge the living and the dead
And in the Holy Ghost, the holy [small "c" catholic] church
The remission of sins, the resurrection of the flesh
The life everlasting.

The addition, *"descendit ad inferna"*—*"He descended into hell"* was added to the Latin version by the priest, Tyrannius Rufinus, of the Aquileian church near Rome in A.D. 404. This is a clear indication that the doctrine of Plato's immortal soul had by this time crept into the Church. The argument went as follows: Jesus, as the Son of Man, was assumed to have had an immortal soul and, as a conscious entity, He would have departed from the dead body. After His Resurrection, Jesus Himself had said to Mary that He had not yet ascended to His Father (John 20:17) so there was really only one alternative place for Him to have been and "*descended into hell*" was added to the Creed. An appeal was made to 1 Peter 3:19-20 to support this but there has been scholarly contention about this teaching for centuries. In 1962 the Church of England changed the words to "*He descended to the dead.*" Nevertheless, by rehearsal at each service for sixteen-hundred years the idea of the soul leaving the body to go to another place has become firmly established as part of the Christian belief system.

The penultimate line in the original Greek Creed reads "*resurrection of the flesh* [*sarx*]" whereas Scripture is very specific and reads, "*resurrection of the dead* [*nekros*]." Recognizing that the Creed is not the Word of God, Church authorities have, over the centuries, changed a number of words and no doubt this practice will continue until the Second Coming. For several centuries the Church of England prayer book used three variant endings of the Apostles' Creed: "The flesh" for the baptism of infants, "the dead" for the Eucharist and "the body" for the daily office. There was a slight change some years ago when the Apostles' Creed in the Eucharist was replaced by the Nicene Creed that makes no mention of where Jesus went and correctly speaks of resurrection of the dead.

Out-of Body Experiences [OBE's]

We saw in the previous chapter that Plato had been impressed by the account of the young man, Er, and there have certainly been many such accounts since that time. This author has interviewed individuals, Christian and non-Christian, who have had an OBE including abduction in a UFO, and there is no question that to the individual these experiences are absolutely real and often life-changing. Paul speaks about such an experience in the following terms:

2 Corinthians 12:1-4

> I will come to visions and revelations of the Lord ... And I know such a man—whether in the body, or out of the body, I do not know, God knows—how he was caught up into

> paradise, and heard inexpressible words, which it is not
> lawful [i.e. proper] for a man to utter.

This passage is sometimes referred to as "Paul's Vision" and there is
an apocryphal account of what he saw supposedly written by Paul
himself and sealed in an alabaster box. It has never been accepted
as true. Most commentators do agree that Paul is obscurely referring to himself in this passage but it makes little difference to the
fact that it is used in a teaching to demonstrate that the soul can
leave the body. It is therefore separable suggesting that it is immortal. Of course, God is sovereign and can give those He so choses visions or even transport them bodily. There are several examples in
Scripture: Moses who saw the tabernacle in heaven (Hebrews 8:5),
Isaiah (6:1) who saw the throne of heaven, Ezekiel (8:3 and 11:24)
who had visions of God, Philip who was carried away bodily from
near Jerusalem to Azotus (Acts 8:39-40) and John of Patmos who
saw visions of horses and was carried away in the Spirit (Revelation
9:17 and 17:3).

Nevertheless, Paul speaks of these experiences as visions and reve-
lations as do Ezekiel, Daniel, Peter and Luke of Paul in Acts 16:9
and 18:9. None of them claim they had left their body so that these
cannot be said to be out-of-body or soul-travel experiences. Certainly none of them had anything to do with death. Paul used the
word "heaven" then repeated his statement using the word "paradise." This word was borrowed from the Persian and originaly referred to the Garden of Eden but in Paul's time had come to be
synonymous with heaven. However, Paul's last words in this passage
are very significant for Christians today. Among the early Christians
there were those who reported mystic experiences and these had a
disasterous effect upon the Church. Sir Edward Burnett Tylor, the
founder of cultural anthropology, records many accounts of those
who had supposedly visited hell and he makes the observation that
by the fourth century A.D. these accounts had taken hold of Christian belief.[1] We saw that above in the case of the Apostles' Creed.

From the mid-nineteenth century there have been an increasing
number of individuals who report near-death-experiences [NDE's]
and out-of-body experiences [OBE's]. The number of well documented cases is now so enormous that it has been necessary to set
up an international forum for the exchange of research findings.[2]
One of the best books to provide an analysis of these accounts from
the medical and Christian perspective has been provided by Dr.
Leon Greene, a cardiologist, professor of medicine and Christian.[3]

He cautions that many of these modern accounts of visits to heaven have been reported by non-Christians including Buddhists while at least two are a flagrant attempt to promote Mormonism.

Among others reporting these experiences are genuine Christians. One well known example is Betty Maltz who has been on the North American Christian television talk circuit as a popular speaker for years. Her account of dying on the operating table, being covered over with a sheet and speaking of a death certificate being issued while her soul/spirit was in heaven for 28 minutes has fascinated viewers and her readers for years. While she is sincerely convinced of having had the experience, an investigation of the medical records showed that she had had a perfectly normal appendectomy, did not die, was not covered over with a sheet and there was no death certificate.[4] While her experience consisted of going to the gates of heaven the question is, as a Christian, should she be talking about it? According to Paul, definitely not—"*it is not lawful* [i.e. proper] *for a man to utter*"—and the reason is not difficult to find. Every one of these accounts reinforces the belief in Plato's separable and immortal soul with heaven for believers and non-believers alike. The resurrection and judgment are thus made redundant and the original lie is confirmed. It takes little discernment to know where these counterfeit experiences originate. In virtually all of them, including Plato's account of Er, the spirit guide instructs the spiritual voyager to go back and relate his experience to others.

The Doctrine of Purgatory

The doctrine of purgatory came directly from these out-of-body accounts. In his *De Anima* [The Soul], second century Church Father, Tertullian, gave an account of a soul claimed to have been seen by a Montanist sister.[5] Tertullian became convinced that the soul separated from the body after death. In the fourth century Augustine stretched a passage from Malachi 3:1-6 and suggested in his *City of God* that, "*some ... shall suffer some kind of purgatorial punishments.*" He offered a familiar passage from Scripture to support his statement: [6]

1 Corinthians 3:12-15

> Now if anyone builds on this foundation with gold, silver, precious stones, wood, hay, straw, each one's work will become manifest; for the day will declare it, because it will be revealed by fire; and the fire will test each one's work, of what sort it is. If anyone's work which he has built on it endures, he will receive a reward. If anyone's work is

burned, he will suffer loss; but he himself will be saved, yet so as through fire.

In his *Ecclesiastical History of the English People* completed in A.D. 696, the Venerable Bede gave a long and detailed account by Dryhthelm, a Christian man who had died then revived a short time later. He told of being led to a horrible valley, ice on one side and fire on the other and the souls of men being thrown from side to side. He thought it was hell but his guide explained that this was a place of torment to purge and purify the unconfessed sins of Christian souls before entry to heaven. He added that the fastings, the prayers and especially the alms of the living would shorten the time for the suffering dead in this place. Thus, was the idea of purgatory introduced to the people of England.[7] In A.D. 885 a similar experience of being taken to the fiery valley befell Charles III, king of the West Franks [France], and Monarch of the Roman Empire. Charles III, the Fat, thus promoted the idea of purgatory among the Continental Europeans.[8] Many accounts are recorded: In A.D. 1196 a monk of Evesham, England, saw the soul of his father being thrown into fire then into ice and there is even a record that the prophet Mohammad had such such an experience.[9] Much later, the Russian Orthodox Church also received accounts of OBE's that eventually led to their doctrine of the seven houses of temptation that the Christian must successfully navigate in order to enter heaven. None of this is found in Scripture.

The entire scene of purgatory and hell with all their torments were gloriously promoted by the thirteenth century Italian poet, Dante Alighieri, in his very long narrative poem *Divina Comedia*. The theme of the poem concerns a man who was given a conducted tour of the Inferno [Hell], of Purgatorio [Purgatory] and of Paradise. His guide through the Inferno and Purgatorio was the long-dead Roman poet, Virgil. In the Inferno he sees that it is a place of the damned while in the Purgatorio he sees repentant Christian sinners being purged of their sins. In this work Dante had lifted the Greek ideas about *hades* directly from Virgil's *Aeneid* who in turn had lifted much from Plato's *Phaedrus* and combined it with misused Scripture to produce a work that virtually came to have the authority of Scripture itself.[10]

In northern Europe an anonymous written work describing purgatory supposedly told by Lazarus after his resuscitation was published in Holland in 1484. Known as the Vision of Tundale[11] this work described the torments in purgatory as happening in the

Dante Alighieri (1265–1321) author of *Divina Comedia.* Unrequited love for Beatrice, a young lady who died at an early age, was the inspiration for Dante who, through his poem, sought to find her by means of his spirit guide, Virgil. [Metro Toronto Reference Library]

present rather than at some time in the future and thus made prayers for the dead more imminent. The Dutch painter, Hieronymus Bosch, was inspired by the Vision of Tundale and produced his *Ascent of the Blessed* showing the ascent of the saints to heaven in the "tunnel of light." Many people today having had a near death experience report this same or a very similar vision.[12]

The idea of purgatory slipped into the Church gradually, was formally introduced by Gregory the Great in A.D. 593 but it did not become official dogma until the Council of Florence in 1439. By that time it was based upon tradition. The bottom line is that these OBE accounts have served to continually reinforce the belief by Christians in Plato's separable soul throughout the past two thousand years. The third place of destiny for the soul, purgatory, still remains secure as part of Vatican II.[13]

Praying for the Dead

The early pre-Reformation Church Fathers paid respect to Augustine and found Jewish tradition and the Jewish book of Maccabees to support the doctrine of purgatory and prayers for the dead. Judas Maccabeus (died 160 B.C.) was a Jewish guerilla fighter at the time of the Syrian occupation of Israel. The history of this war was recorded in the two books of Maccabees. In the second book there is a passage (12:38–45) where Maccabeus, who believed in the resurrection, prayed for those of his men who had died, *"It is therefore a holy and wholesome thought to pray for the dead that they may be loosed from sins."* (verse 45). By including this book and passage in their canon of Scripture, the early Church had Scriptural authority for praying for their dead. It has remained in the Roman Catholic Bibles but was not included in the Protestant Bibles.

The requirement to pray for the dead led to some burial practices that step by step caused public health problems in the cities and later justification to introduce the practice of cremation. It began with the Crusades in the eleventh and twelfth centuries. We saw in Chapter One that the wealthy Crusaders often supported the local monastic order and under these circumstances it was not too difficult to persuade the Abbot to allow the body of the dead hero to be buried in his lead-lined coffin beneath the abbey altar. The argument went that since the hero had died fighting for Christ he thereby became one of the "special dead," a martyr, and thus eligible for priviledged burial beneath the altar. Justification relied upon the following passages:

Revelation 6:9
> John in heaven: I saw under the altar the souls of
> those who had been slain for the Word of God ...

Revelation 20:8
> John in heaven: And I saw the souls of those who
> Had been beheaded for their witness to Jesus ...

Of course, burial beneath the altar had definite advantages. With a suitable endowment, often actually engraved in stone on the casket lid, the priest and those who followed him would have this before them as a reminder as they stood at the altar mouthing the appropriate prayers over the body in perpetuity. Thus freed from the certain unfaithfulness of relatives, the deceased had a virtual guarantee of shortened time in purgatory. With the "martyr-crusader" securely in place beneath the abbey altar, other family members soon began to seek an adjacent spot that they felt would be a protected resting place for their own souls; burial *ad sanctos*. A generous endowment usually eased their passage to a nearby spot beneath the chancel floor. The Church authorities made huge sums of money by permitting the bodies of the wealthy to be placed within the church. New churches were then built with extensive crypts to hold more bodies and, of course, all this represented considerable endowment income. Each and every body buried within the church building had to be in a stout, gas-tight wooden coffin. Whether those coffins were beneath floor level or above it as is the case in say, Westminster Abbey, the body does not return to the earth and is thus, in reality, a non-burial.

Finally, with the belief in purgatory firmly established and the necessity of prayers for the dead, the doctrine of indulgences was introduced. This practice began with good Christian intention but step by step badly departed from it. It is generally agreed that Thomas Aquinas in the thirteenth century invented the scheme known as the Paid-Up Capital of the Bank of Indulgences. There was a complicated balance sheet of sins, penances, prayers and payments. It was even possible for the wealthy to pay in advance for sins anticipated! The entire corrupt scheme eventually led to the Reformation of 1517. However, we should be reminded that it was out-of-body experiences that led to the doctrines of purgatory, prayers for the dead and the scandal of indulgences. Those out-of-body experiences also sustained the belief in the separable and immortal soul and continue to do so to this day in almost all Church denominations.

The Resurrection Bone

In the Middle Ages a straw-man argument that would attempt to undermine the belief in the resurrection was inadvertently set up by the theologians. Paul's analogy of the seed to explain the resurrection, given in his first letter to the Corinthians and mentioned in his second letter, was taken quite literally:

1 Corinthians 15:36-38
> Foolish one, what you sow is not made alive unless it dies. And what you sow, you do not sow that body that shall be, but mere grain—perhaps wheat ...

2 Corinthians 1:21-22
> Now He who ... has anointed us is God, who also has sealed us and given us the Spirit in our hearts as a deposit.

A common belief then grew up among Christians that the human body contained a "resurrection bone"—generally thought to be a pea-sized bone—that did not decay but remained as the "seed" for the new resurrection body. This is one reason that burning was the chosen death for the heretic. For them it was the most fearful since not only was it the most painful exit from this life but it removed all possibility for the next. About the year 1300, a papal decretal forbade the dissection of Christian bodies in the belief that this would interfere with the resurrection. This greatly retarded the understanding of human anatomy for over two hundred years. Eventually, the great Belgian anatomist, Andreas Vesalius (1514–1564), decided to search for the elusive "resurrection bone." It was a risky business—he had to steal a body from a gibbet outside Louvain—but nevertheless he publically demonstrated its absence. Thus, by dismissing the resurrection bone the resurrection itself was cast into doubt. Nevertheless, the belief in the resurrection bone lingered on into the nineteenth century.[14]

Ashes to Ashes ...

One of the interesting little steps taken to establish the practice of cremation among Christians took place over three hundred years before Dr. Price's outrage of 1884. The Church of England's Book of Common Prayer was first published for King Edward the sixth in 1549 and the well-known burial prayer reads in part: *"I commende thy soul to God the Father Almighty, and thy body to the grounde, earth to earth, ashes to ashes, dust to dust, in sure and certain hope of resurrection to eternal life ... "* While at the time this may have been intended to accommodate those who had died in a fire, the Puritans of the day recognized that not all these words were from Scripture. Adam was not created from a preadamic ash-heap. The Puritan version[15] of this same passage of the burial prayer was issued in 1618 and reads: *"... we therefore commit his body to the earth, in certain hope of resurrection to eternal life ... "* At that time, cremation as a means of body disposal for the Christian public, would never have been contemplated. Yet the well-known words rehearsed from the Book of Common prayer, *"ashes to ashes, dust to dust"* are heard today at every disposal service whether public, private or a scene in movies and television. Those words contain some Scripture, are perceived by many to be entirely Scriptural and have very effectively promoted the notion, even among clergy, that cremation is sanctioned by the Bible.

Ash Wednesday

The Roman Church is very much guided by tradition and the tradition throughout Christendom has been disposal by burial. Burning was reserved for enemies of the Church. The steps taken to turn this mindset around were thus carried out over a very long period of time although it is not being suggested here that it was deliberately planned. The *"ashes to ashes ..."* statement in the Church of

England Prayer Book appeared in 1549 and the theologians at that time presumably had no idea that their words would be effectively used three centuries later to promote cremation. The Ash Wednesday tradition in both the Roman Church and the Church of England certainly began many centuries ago and is still carried out to this day although it will not be found in Scripture. The use of ashes in Scripture is associated with mourning. On Ash Wednesday, about six weeks prior to Easter, in the ceremony called "imposition," the priest places the mark of the cross upon the forehead of the faithful with his finger using blessed ashes. The object is to stress penitance, as distinct from repentance, and Genesis 3:19 and Joel 2:12-13 are quoted. The Genesis verse "*Remember man, that thou art dust, and unto dust you shall return*" nicely establishes in the minds of the people that ashes and dust are one and the same thing. Thus, in being cremated and finishing as ashes, this is perceived to be according to Scripture. The Joel verse "*... with fasting and with weeping and with mourning; so rend your heart and not your garments ...*" has no mention of ashes except in the Roman Bible where the word "ashes" has been added after the word "mourning". A religious ceremony involving ashes very effectively makes it right in the minds of the penitants that they may, with the Church's blessing, depart in the fires of purification and finish as ashes.

Scattering Cremated Ashes

The Church of England has increasingly adopted the practice of scattering the ashes of the deceased with an appropriate dedicatory prayer. The ashes may be scattered—they prefer the word "strewn"—in an area set aside for this purpose in the public cemetery garden; special requests may call for scattering at sea or over the local golf course. The Bishop of Woolwich, Rt. Rev. R.W. Stannard writing in the *Church Times* in 1958 put his finger squarely on the reason for the growing practice of scattering ashes by the Church. He pointed out that the cremation chapel, directly associated with the furnace, has increasingly replaced the church building as the location for the disposal service—one hesitates to call it a burial service. Thus, not only are the cemetery grounds no longer under the purview of the Church, but in the case of a cremation, the service itself is no longer held in the church. Bishop Stannard suggested that the body be cremated first and the ashes taken in an urn to the church for the service, then scattered on a rose garden in the consecrated ground of the church precincts.[16] What is actually being said here is a rather sad attempt to regain the Church's lost authority pertaining to the destiny of the soul, the disposal of the mortal remains and just possibly, a matter of revenue. At the time Bishop Stannard was writing (1958), 30 per cent of those who died in Great Britain were cremated; that figure today has more than doubled.

If the Church had any understanding of Scripture or history they would recall the dozens of cases of Christian martyrs who died in the flames for their faith then had their ashes scattered by their pagan persecutors. Their persecutors' declared object was to "destroy their resurrection" but this is refuted by the words of Jesus:

Luke 12:4

> My friends, do not be afraid of those who kill the body,
> and after that have no more that they can do.

John Wycliffe, a name known to every Christian, died a natural death in 1384 then the Roman monks finally located his body in 1428, burned the bones and scattered the ashes in Lutterworth Brook. William Tyndale was strangled, burned at the stake and his ashes scattered in 1536. Jan Huss was burned and his ashes scattered in the Rhine in 1415. At least two Scripture passages give precedence for this practice: Exodus 32:20 and Deuteronomy 9:21. In both passages Moses took the abominable golden calf that the Israelites had made, burned it with fire, crushed it to dust and threw the dust into the brook. In doing precisely the same thing with the Christian dead the Church is in effect treating them as something abominable by providing the obsequies of the heretic and the murderer!

Fear of Premature Burial

One of the less than subtle means of promoting the practice of cremation was to literally frighten people into making this choice by horror stories of being buried alive. Taphiphobia is the wonderful word given to this fear. Fiction writer Edgar Allan Poe (1809–1849) wrote no less than eight short horror stories including *The Premature Burial* and the more famous *The Pit and the Pendulum* in which the theme was the horror of being buried alive.[17] Swedish industrialist Alfred Nobel (1833–1896) suffered from claustropobia and his greatest and only petition was not to be buried alive.[18] He funded a Foundation for the Propagation of Cremation in Paris in 1880 and planned to use his fortune for the construction of crematoria all over Europe. Opposition from the Roman Catholic Church forced him for find another way to use his money and the world finished up with the famous Nobel prizes.[19]

John Wycliffe (1330–1384) English reformer was student and professor at Oxford University for over 30 years. Although influenced by Augustine he developed a systematic attack on the hierarchical church system, doctrines of purgatory, penances and transubstantiation. In 1380 he enlisted a body of "pore priests" later known as Lollards. He began a translation of the Bible. His works were rigidly repressed and burnt. [Metro Toronto Reference Library]

Wycliffe minced no words when it came to the Latin Church. He referred to the friars as *fend on helle* [fiend from hell]. He died a natural death and 44 years later (in 1428) following an order given by the Council of Constance, his bones were exhumed, burned, and the ashes scattered in the Lutterworth River to "destroy his resurrection." [Leonard Library, Wycliffe College, Toronto]

Arthur Hallam edited a quarterly journal having the title *The Burial Reformer*. The first volume appeared in April 1905, continued until December 1908 then continued under the title *Perils of Premature Burial*. This periodical and several books and numerous magazine articles all recounted one horrific incident after another.[20] Disinterred corpses were claimed to be found with excessive hair and finger nail growth and even a half-chewed shroud in the mouth. All these purported evidences of the victim having been buried alive were guaranteed to leave the unanswered questions in the mind of the reader: how many more are there out there and will I be one of them? Most of these stories were complete fabrications since the air available in a sealed coffin is only sufficient for an hour or so. Nevertheless, they all appeared at about the same time in both North America and in Europe. This was precisely the period when the Cremation Societies were most actively promoting the practice. As these stories began to be circulated among the public many began to be convinced that having the body drained of blood [ex-sanguination] and cremation might be the quicker and more certain way to go. To this day some people who, in fear of being buried alive, request that their arteries be severed before burial or cremation. The funeral establishment will recommend embalming when such a request is made. There is, of course, an extra fee.

Re-introduction of Spiritualism

A more subtle means of promoting cremation was to remove any fear of "consciousness" during burning by emphasizing the absence of the self from the body. The Greeks and Romans practiced necromancy or spiritualism. This virtually disappeared during the Christian era then received its modern impetus in Europe from mesmerism, i.e. hypnotism, and by 1847 this had become popular in England. Spiritualism was dramatically introduced to the American public the following year, March 31, 1848. This was almost twenty years prior to the Medical International Congress of 1869 and just at the time when belief in evil spirits was fading in the mainline churches. The place was Hydesville, New York, at the cottage of the three Fox sisters where mysterious rapping noises were heard. The sisters learned to communicate with them. These phenomenon attracted journalists from both sides of the Atlantic and caught the world's attention. By the following year there were Spiritualist organizations in the US and the UK that spawned over a dozen periodicals convincing a great number of people that it was possible to contact dead relatives and friends. A direct offshoot of the Hydesville affair was the founding of the "Ghost Society" by Cambridge (UK) theology students E. W. Benson, B. F. Westcott and F. J. A. Hort in 1851. University Societies are seldom long-lived but this one did and was given the more formal name, the Psychical Society and then by 1860 it became the Society for Psychical Research. E. W. Benson went on to become Archbishop of Canterbury, B. F. Westcott became Bishop and F. J. A. Hort became a professor of Divinity. They all remained active members of the Society for years.[21] The Society is based in London and still flourishes while its periodical *Psychic News* is still being published. In all cases, the presumption was, and still is, the survival of the conscious soul in complete and rapturous separation from the decaying body. Yet again, this is just another scheme to promote and sustain the belief that the human soul is immortal.

Just forty years after the founding of the Spiritualist Movement in America, two of the three Fox sisters, who had been the initial driving force behind this Movement, confessed publically that the entire affair had been a fraud.[22] This should have been the death-blow to Spiritualism but by this time so many had been convinced that no one believed them. The Movement continues to this day as the Spiritualist Church. The organization is careful to identify itself with the true Christian Church, although they do not believe in the resurrection, and claim to be at the leading edge of modern Christianity. Running parallel to the spiritual side of the Movement were the scientists who conducted investigations of the strange phenomena with thermometers and measuring tape. Some very eminent Victorian names from the sciences and from literature, were actively involved in scientific investigations but firm conclusions were ever elusive.[23] Today, that work, now dressed in the robes of scientific respectibility and conducted behind the hallowed walls of academia, is called parapsychology.

Cremation "Subverts the Belief in the Resurrection"

Roman Catholic spokesman, Father Dorsett writing at the end of the 1800s, put the matter of the effect of cremation on the bereaved rather succinctly:

> "*Cremation also seems opposed to the sentiments of the thoughtful person who believes man was made in the image of God ... Cremation may almost be said to encroach on the rights of the Creator and anticipate the work of destruction which belongs to Him alone.... If belief in the resurrection of the body is to hold its own in the minds of men we must treat*

Fenton John Anthony Hort, 1828–1892

Edward White Benson, 1829–1896

Brooke Foss Westcott, 1825–1901

As Cambridge theological students these were the founders of the "Ghost Society" in 1851. In 1860 the Society was re-named the Society for Psychical Research and its purpose was to investigate spiritualist manifestations. Westcott and Hort remained as active members for years. [Fisher Rare Book Library & Metro Toronto Reference Library] *the body in such a way as to impress upon their imagination a picture which shall represent preservation and not complete destruction ... Thus, on psychological grounds, cremation tends to subvert the belief of men in the resurrection of the body."* [24]

An interesting admission of the psychological problems with cremation appeared in an article published in the prestigious *The Architectural Review* for April 1967. The author, Peter Bond, complained that in existing crematoria something is missing when the coffin disappears behind a curtain, since it leaves the mourners "hanging." His words are:

"The moment of committal is the climax of the ceremony and of all the relationships which existed between the deceased person and each of the mourners. A social pattern has lost one of its units ... by merely removing the coffin from view ... leaving the mourner's uncertain of the consummation of the ceremony and with a feeling of having left the deceased behind. In earth burial no one fails to recognize the significance of the moment when a coffin is lowered into the ground. Those witnessing it are subject to deep emotional experience ... The reality of that moment has been faced, has been suffered. Present day arrangements allow no such significance to exist in the case of cremation." [25]

This problem of the mourners not seeing the body lowered into the ground was recognized at a very early date when cremation was first introduced. Siemens, the German industrial furnace manufacturer, designed a furnace that could be installed beneath the floor of the chapel so that the coffin could be lowered directly into the incineration chamber. However, as far as is known, this was never built. The reason was undoubtedly because of the inevitable distraction of the noise and escaping fumes and smoke. The reader might wonder how many mourners do suffer psychological problems caused by cremation not fulfilling the natural grieving process. If the truth be known, the cremation process may well be one of the root causes of psychological bereavement problems by engendering an unspoken denial of the resurrection and instilling a sense of hopelessness.

The practices of non-burial, including cremation, is actually disobedience to that early commandment that we return to the dust. In the next few chapters we will attempt to show that non-burial has serious consequences for the living who remain. First, however, there has to be something said about what is actually involved in *"returning to the dust of the ground."*

Siemen's proposed cremation furnace. The proposal was made, though not carried out, to overcome the psychological problems experienced by mourners not seeing the coffin go down into the ground as in earth burial. [Metro Toronto Reference Library]

5

The Life is in the Blood

*... who can be drowsy at the hour which freed us
from everlasting sleep? Or have slumbering thoughts
at that time, when sleep itself must end,
and, as some conjecture, all shall awake again?*

SIR THOMAS BROWNE, *RELIGIO MEDICI.* 1643

The Creation of Man

It is always a good idea to start at the beginning. In this chapter we
need to go back to the creation of man and the animals from the
dust of the ground. The animals were created on the fifth and sixth
days of creation. Adam was also created on the sixth day, just after
all the animals. Eve was the last to be created on that same day but
in her case God did not use the dust of the ground but took a part
of Adam—traditionally, a rib.[1]

There are a number of Scriptural passages that mention the very
ancient custom of throwing dust into the air. Appendix B lists ten
references in Scripture to *"placing oneself under the dust."* Commentators have said that putting dust on the head is supposed to have
been originally intended as a symbol of man's origin from dust, and
conveys the idea of humility. However, putting oneself under a
head-covering, e.g. a hat, is symbolical of being under the authority
represented by that covering and plays an important part in this custom. Paul put it this way:

1 Corinthians 11:10
> "... the woman ought to have a symbol of authority on her
> head [a head covering], because of the [fallen?] angels"

Thus, placing oneself under the dust i.e. by throwing dust in the air,
symbolizes the fact that one day the dust will inevitably have authority over every one of us. There is an example given in Acts 22:23
where the mob *"threw dust into the air"* in reaction to Paul's claim that

God had sent him to the Gentiles. The Jewish crowd was clearly furious at what they perceived to be Paul's arrogance and, by throwing dust on their own heads, gave a symbolic gesture to remind him to be humble since he too would eventually come under the authority of the dust of the ground. Remnants of this practice can still be found today at funeral processions in country areas of the Middle-East where they still throw dust in the air.

Somewhat corrupt versions of this creation account have been found by archaeologists and anthropologists in nations throughout the world and Sir James George Frazer's monumental work *Folklore in the Old Testament* is a veritable goldmine of information. By his own admission Frazer was not a Christian but he was a great scholar. He wrote in beautiful prose and with meticulous documentation.[2] The Babylonians had a legend that their god, Bel, cut off his own head while the other gods caught the blood and mixed it with clay and fashioned man from the mixture. There was an ancient tradition among the Egyptians that, in the infancy of their history as a people, their god Noum had taught their fathers that they were but clay and dust. In another Egyptian legend Khnoumou, the Father of the gods, is said to have molded men out of red clay on his potter's wheel. In Greek legend the Titan, Prometheus, is said to have molded the first men out of clay at Panopeus in Phocis. These legends are not confined to the ancient peoples of the Middle East; similar accounts can be found on the opposite side of the world. The Australian aborigines had a legend that Pund-jel, the Creator, molded two human forms from the clay of the ground then blew his breath hard into their mouths, nostrils and navels and they became living men. The Maoris of New Zealand say that one of their gods, variously named Tiki or Tane, took red riverside clay, mixed it with his own blood and molded an image in exact copy of himself then animated it by breathing into its mouth and nostrils. Similar legends were discovered and recorded by the early explorers before influence by missionary accounts. Frazer also includes accounts from Burma, Polynesia and Siberia of the creation of the first woman from the rib of the first man.[3]

Acknowledging that we came via Adam from the dust of the ground, the expression "Mother Earth" begins to take on a deeper meaning while the otherwise strange line in Psalm 139:15 about our being *"wrought in the lowest parts of the earth"* can be seen to refer to Adam. We have already seen how God commanded Adam to return to the dust of the ground and, as far as Believer's are concerned, this should be the end of all argument about cremation. Nevertheless, in

an attempt to provide an explanation we need to return to the creation account. Here we find that the Hebrew makes less of a distinction between man and the animal kingdom than may appear to be
the case from our English Bible translations:

Genesis 1:24
> Then God said, "Let the earth bring forth the living creature
> [*nephesh*] according to its kind ..."

Genesis 2:7
> And the Lord God formed man of the dust of the ground,
> and breathed into his nostrils the breath of life;
> and man became a living being [*nephesh*].

Michaelangelo's depiction of the creation of Adam in the fourth
panel on the Sistine Chapel ceiling is not the way Adam was created! God had called the atomic particles together to form Adam
then breathed into the nostrils and he became a *nephesh*. In the case
of the animals, the record does not say that God breathed into
them, nevertheless, they also became a *nephesh*. The word *nephesh* is
used for both animals and man and, while usually translated "soul,"
the NKJV translators above have chosen to use the words "living
creature" in the case of the animals and "living being" in the case of
man. One reason the translators made this choice was undoubtedly
to make a clear separation between the two kingdoms. In this way,
there would be no hint of evolution between one kingdom and the
other. While Scripture does not support evolution of any kind, the
Hebrew *nephesh*, makes no distinction between man and beast. Further evidence that man and beast have much in common is that the
Hebrew shows both to have a *ruach* or spirit:

Ecclesiastes 3:21
> Who knows the spirit [*ruach*] of the sons of man,
> which goes upward, and the spirit [*ruach*] of the beast,
> which goes down to the earth?

This is simply to say that both man and animal originated from the
dust of the ground, each has a *nephesh* [soul] and each has a *ruach*
[spirit]. However, it is emphasized that while there are these com-
monalities between man and beast, man was made in God's image
and likeness and it is this that sets him well apart from the animal
kingdom.

Blood, the Interface of Body and Soul

There are several places in Scripture where we are told that the *nephesh* is in the blood. In some instances *nephesh* is translated "life," thus, the life is in the blood. This applies to both man and beast and this fact is important when we consider that animals were used for the atonement sacrifices. The atonement principle was first demonstrated by God Himself in the Garden of Eden where He "*made tunics of skin, and clothed them*" (Genesis 3:21). This verse is almost cryptic but from verses that follow it becomes clear that one of the flock, probably a lamb, was killed and blood shed to provide the skin. Upon leaving the Ark, Noah was given permission to eat meat but not its life, that is, its blood (Genesis 9:4). It is not until the Book of Leviticus that we discover that the life is in the blood and an explanation of the atonement principle given:

Leviticus 17:11

> For the life [*nephesh*] of the flesh is in the blood, and I have given it to you upon the altar to make atonement for your souls; for it is the blood that makes atonement for the soul.

The atoning sacrifice is the process of giving one life on behalf of another, in this case the sacrifice of an animal life for the life of man. A life for a life, or, a soul for a soul. In the Old Testament this was the highest form of sacrifice possible. The animal was to be a perfect specimen "*without blemish*" while, of course unlike man, the animal kingdom was of itself not fallen but merely living in the cursed world of fallen man. From this aspect, the life of the animal was of greater "spiritual purity" than that of man and thus more acceptable to God as the sacrifice. While human sacrifice is not being suggested here, a perfect man, not fallen, would be the perfect sacrifice. Adam was initially perfect but made a free-will choice to disobey God. A little insight into the unfallen nature of the animal kingdom concerns instinct. Many scientists argue from an evolutionary position and claim that the animal kingdom has no free will but operates by instinct. However, the catch-all word "instinct" may sound scientific but it is not well understood. God has told us that He has written His laws in our hearts [conscience] and reasonably "instinct" is simply that the animals more obediently follow God's direction. For example, animal and bird migration is still largely a mystery.

The Levitical statement (17:11) above concerning the sacrificial atonement is immediately followed by a further instruction related to the disposition of the blood:

Leviticus 17:13-14:
>And whatever man ... who hunts and catches any animal or
>bird that may be eaten, he shall pour out its blood and cover
>it with dust; for it is the life [*nephesh*] of all flesh. Its blood
>sustains its life [*nephesh*]. Therefore ... you shall not eat the
>blood of any flesh, for the life [*nephesh*] of all flesh is its
>blood. Whoever eats it will be cut off.

Deuteronomy 12:24
>You shall not eat it [the blood]; you shall pour it out on the
>earth like water.

The principle of returning the blood containing the life [*nephesh*] to
the ground is repeated over twenty-four times in Scripture and by
this emphasis it is surely one of utmost importance. These are listed
in Appendix B. Strangely however, each of those Scripture passages
give the impression that the disposal of the blood "*at the side of the altar*" is a minor detail whereas it is, in fact, the atonement process.
The business with the kidneys, etc. on top of the altar usually gets all
the attention and we might be tempted to suggest that all the detail
given for this part of the sacrifice was a distraction. The only reason
we are given for the burning on top of the altar was to provide "*a
sweet smelling savor.*"

The first mention of blood returning to the ground is in Genesis:

Genesis 4:10
>And He [God] said, "What have you [Cain] done? The voice
>of your brother's [Abel] blood cries out to Me from the
>ground."

Genesis 15:10
>Then he [Abram] brought all these [heifer, goat, ram,
>turtledove and pigeon] to Him and cut them in two, down
>the middle, and he placed each piece opposite the other;

Although this passage concerning Abram is not too specific, obvi-
ously a lot of blood was shed since God was able to walk between the
divided parts. Thus, there was no altar and the blood returned to
the dust of the earth. Noah and Abram each built an altar to make
an animal sacrifice, but it is not until the Book of Exodus that we are
given some detail about the altar's construction. Although illus-
trated Bibles often show the altars of Noah and Abram in terms of

The atonement sacrifice in the Old Testament required strong young men to handle the animals and ensure that their soul returned to the earth by means of the blood discharged into the gutter at the base of the altar. [Drawing by Elizabeth Roth]

that described for use in the Exodus, it turns out that the early altars were made of earth or uncut stone. God evidently regards the return of life to the dust of the ground so highly that He wants nothing that has been defiled by the hand of man, such as a cut stone, to receive the life:

Exodus 20:24-26

An altar of earth you shall make for Me, and you shall sacrifice on it your burnt offerings and your peace offerings … And if you make Me an altar of stone, you shall not build it of hewn stone; for if you use your tool on it, you have profaned it. Nor shall you go up by steps to My altar, that your nakedness may not be exposed on it.

Specific details for making the portable altar for use during the journey from Egypt and the animal sacrifices are given in the Book of Exodus then repeated in Leviticus. While some of the animal parts were burnt upon the altar, the bulk of the blood amounting to dozens of litres in the case of a bull, were always poured out "*against the altar.*"

Exodus 29:12

> You shall take some of the blood of the bull and put it on the
> horns of the altar with your finger, and pour all the blood
> beside the base of the altar.

Leviticus 1:15

> The priest shall bring it [turtledove or pigeon] to the altar,
> wring off its head, and burn it on the altar; its blood shall be
> drained out at the side of the altar.

A further nineteen passages from Levitus repeat the instruction to
pour out the animal blood by the side of the altar. See Appendix
B. Returning the blood—the life—to the ground is therefore related to the physical creation of the animal from the ground in
the beginning. Considering the emphasis placed upon returning
animal blood to the ground, one may wonder how much more important this was and still is, for human blood? As we have seen earlier, the history of human body disposal has been one of
deliberate and determined effort to oppose that early commandment given to Adam. It may also begin to be evident that the opposition is more specifically directed to preventing the blood from
returning to the ground. For example, in the increasingly popular
embalming process, the blood is drained into the city sewer! According to Scripture there are serious consequences resulting
from not permitting the blood to return to the ground, that is,
non-burial.

The Unique Case of Burning the Blood.

This sacrifice is concerned with the red heifer. It is different from all
the other sacrifices and can be more closely identified with the cremation process. This is the only case where the whole of the blood
and thus the life itself was burned; it is described in Numbers 19:1-9.
God instructed Moses to slaughter a flawless red heifer [young cow]
outside the camp then in verses 4-5.

Numbers 19:4-5

> Eleazar [third son of Aaron] the priest shall take some of its
> blood [the red heifer] with his finger, and sprinkle some of
> its blood seven times directly in front of the tabernacle of
> meeting. Then the heifer shall be burned in his sight: its
> hide, its flesh, its blood, and its offal shall be burned.

The slaughter of the animal for this sacrifice was done outside the camp or, later, outside the temple. In each case, according to the order given in Leviticus 17:3-5, the blood of the animal would not have been poured out onto the ground because this was remote from the door of the tent of meeting.

Leviticus 17:3-5

> Whatever man of the house of Israel who kills an ox or lamb or goat in the camp, or who kills it outside the camp, and does not bring it to the door of the tabernacle of meeting to offer an offering to the Lord before the tabernacle of the Lord, blood guilt shall be imputed to that man ... that man shall be cut off.

In some way, the sacrificial animal was slaughtered and a token of its blood was taken with the finger and sprinkled seven times. Then the entire animal was cut up and burned together with cedar wood, hyssop and scarlet until only ashes remained. Here we have to conclude that the life in the blood finished in the ashes or may have returned to God as a combustion product but certainly it did not return to the ground. However, for the purpose to which these ashes were intended we might be inclined to agree with nineteenth century commentators Keil and Delitzsch that the life remained in the ashes. This is a sobering thought for human cremation.

The remaining verses of Leviticus chapter 19 instruct the Israelites to use a portion of these ashes to produce the waters of purification. These waters were for cleansing those special cases where persons have become unclean or defiled by coming into contact with the dead. Contact with the dead was the strongest of all religious defilements and while plain water was specified for lesser defilements, the waters of purification i.e. containing the ashes of the red heifer, were necessary to cleanse those defiled by the dead. Again, Keil and Delitzsch[4] make the point that plain water was insufficient to cleanse this type of defilement and, as a sin offering, it was necessary to add a reagent they refer to as an "holy alkali." This refers to the ashes derived from a sacrifice that was large [cattle], in the fullness of life [a young female] and in its greatest freshness and vigor [mature and nubile] as a most powerful antidote to death. When the Israelites, under King David, finally had a capital city built and a permanent temple rather than the tabernacle, a special place outside the city was set aside where the red heifer was to be slaughtered and burnt. It is believed that this place was on top of the

Mount of Olives where the priest at the temple could see the heifer being burned on the other side of the Kidron Valley.

From this brief excursion into the business of the animal sacrifices, we are reminded that it was all carried out by the Levite priests in obedience to God's command. Moreover, with hundreds of litres of blood being poured out at the side of the altar, some consideration must have been given to its location. We can only surmise that during the exodus from Egypt the priests were led to a rock fissure of some sort where the blood could drain away. Without this, the entire area would quickly have become a quagmire and the altar slowly begin to sink into it. The sacrificial duties of the Old Testament were clearly a shockingly messy business requiring the strongest of men to wrestle those animals to their death. Just reflecting on this should make us thankful that the New Testament made these practices no longer necessary. However, the principles involved are still valid. In the next chapter we will see the consequences of not returning the blood, that is the soul, to the dust of the ground.

6

Defiling the Land

I shall die as my fathers died,
And sleep as they sleep; even so.
For the glass of the year is brittle
Wherein we gaze for a span

A. C. SWINBURNE, HYMN TO PROSERPINE. 1866

Non-Burial and Defiling of the Land

There are a number of Old Testament verses that warn the reader that certain behaviour causes the land to be defiled. Two Hebrew words are used, *chaneph* and *tame,* both of which have been translated as "defiled." Following the Fall of man, God cursed the ground (Genesis 3:17) but in His mercy to us, when we are obedient, He blesses the ground and limits the curse.[1] However, defiling the land appears to lift God's blessing and permit the curse to have full reign:

Isaiah 24:5-6

> The earth is defiled under its inhabitants, because they have transgressed the laws, changed the ordinance, broken the everlasting covenant. Therefore the curse has devoured the earth ... and the inhabitants of the earth are burned [i.e. punished].

Hosea 4:1-3

> There is no truth or mercy or knowledge of God in the land. By swearing and lying, killing and stealing and committing adultery, they break all restraint, with bloodshed after bloodshed. Therefore the land will mourn; and everyone who dwells there will waste away ...

Worship of other gods [spiritual adultery], murder, sexual adultery, sexual sins of all kinds and, perhaps strangely, non-burial, that is, disobedience to the command given in the Garden of Eden, all contribute to defilement of the land. The following are examples of defilement, first by murder then by non-burial:

Genesis 4:12

God to Cain after he had murdered Abel:
"When you till the ground, it shall no longer yield its strength to you."

Numbers 35:33-34

So you shall not pollute the land where you are; for blood defiles the land, and no atonement can be made for the land, for the blood that is shed upon it, except by the blood of him [the murderer] who shed it.

Deuteronomy 21:22-23

If a man has committed a sin worthy of death, and he is put to death, and you hang him on a tree, his body shall not remain overnight on the tree, but you shall surely bury him that day, so that you do not defile the land which the Lord thy God is giving you as an inheritance; for he who is hanged is accursed of God.

When we consider hanging on a tree, giving to the birds of the air and the beasts of the field, these are also cases of non-burial or more specifically preventing the blood, that is the soul, from returning to the ground. There are found to be a formidable list of twenty-two Scriptures from Genesis to Revelation describing non-burial as a punishment. Two more are given below and the remainder in Appendix B.

Genesis 40:18-19

Joseph to the baker: "This is the interpretation of it [your dream]: The three baskets are three days. Within three days Pharoah will lift off your head from you and hang you on a tree; and the birds will eat your flesh from you."

Ecclesiastes 6:3

If a man begets a hundred children, and lives many years, ... or indeed he has no burial; I say that a stillborn child is better than he.

Revelation 11:9

> Then those from the peoples, ... will see their dead bodies
> three and a half days, and not allow their dead bodies to be
> put in graves.

The prophet Ezekiel in exile in Babylon had some strong words for
the people of the city of Jerusalem. God spoke through Ezekiel and
gave the people notice that judgement would be brought upon the
city because "*her blood is in her midst.*" Verses 6 to 8:

Ezekiel 24:1-14

> Woe to the bloody city [Jerusalem] ... For her blood is in
> her midst. She set it on top of a rock; she did not pour it on
> the ground, to cover it with dust. That it may raise up fury
> and take vengeance, I [God] have set her blood on top of a
> rock that it may not be covered.

The remaining verses in that chapter tell how the people would be
taken into exile so quickly that, like Ezekiel and his wife, there will be
no time to mourn for their dead. Following this, the city itself would
then be destroyed. These very things did happen at the time of the second exile. In their commentary, theologians Keil and Delitzsch,[2] suggest that the city was full of murderers and while this may or may not be
true, the reason given in the verse above is that the blood did not return
to the ground, that is, it was not covered with dust. A possible explanation is that burial was being carried out using stone caskets in which the
blood would be retained. The use of stone caskets by the wealthy was actually a practice that became a tradition among the Jews long before
the time of Christ. Hundreds of stone caskets of Orthodox Jews of more
recent vintage can be seen today in the Kidron Valley outside Jerusalem's east wall. Nevertheless, whatever was actually happening in Ezekiel's time, it was a situation that involved non-burial of blood.

From the earliest classical literature, say from the fifth century B.C.,
there is a recognition of the importance of proper burial. From the
early Greeks, Homer and Sophocles to the Romans, Juvenal and Virgil,
there are dozens of references that consistently refer to non-burial as
punishment. The following are two examples from the classic literature: Sophocles, the 5th century B.C. Greek poet, in his tradgedy *Antigone*, tells how the wicked King Creon ordered the dead body of the
hero, Polinices, to remain unburied. Polinices sister, Antigone, dis-
obeyed the king's decree, covered her brother's dead body, and in her
defense said:

Stone caskets fill the hill-side outside of Jerusalem's East wall in the Kidron Valley. [Photo by author]

Sophocles—Lines 450-459

... nor deemed I that thy decrees were of such force, that a mortal could override the unwritten and unfailing statutes of heaven. For their life is not of today or yesterday, but from all time, and no man knows when they were first put forth.[3]

The Jews certainly knew when "*they were first put forth*"—those statutes of heaven came from the Creator and this particular one was recorded in Genesis 3:19.

Diodorus of Sicily, the first century B.C. historian, explained how after embalming the dead, the Egyptians would be careful to bury except if the dead were found to have debts or be convicted of some horrid crime. In this case they would be denied common burial until the family members made proper restitution.[4]

Non-burial is seen throughout to be a kind of posthumous punishment. When the body is eaten by birds or beasts, the result is that the blood, or what remains of it, is scattered and does not enter the ground. We saw in Chapter One that the Zoroastrians of Persia dispose of their dead by leaving them exposed on "towers of silence" to be eaten by the birds. The end result is that the blood is scattered throughout the surrounding countryside. This was at the center of an amusing debate in the British House of Commons regarding a

Zoroastrian "Tower of Silence." The bodies are laid around the top of the tower and eaten by birds. The remaining bones are later swept into the centre of the tower. A fine example of non-burial. [Metro Toronto Reference Library]

petition by the Zoroastrian community in Britain for permission to build their towers of silence. The petition was denied on the grounds that the English countryside would be littered with the remains of the dead as they passed through the birds! The modern trend to embalm before burial or cremation is surely another example of non-burial where the blood with its essential element, the soul, is "scattered" in the city sewers. We have seen earlier that the ashes of burnt heretics and martyrs were deliberately scattered for the purpose of "spoiling the resurrection," however, we know this to have been a misguided intention. Non-burial and especially burning, were normally seen to be a curse and a punishment. Generally overlooked however, is that burning and scattering are actions of non-burial that defile the land. This is therefore the more important matter since it concerns the living who were left behind rather than the dead. We need to now look particularly at burning as a punishment and as non-burial.

Burning of the Living and the Dead

Before commenting upon burning of the dead we need to say a word about burning of the living. Being burned alive is said to be the most painful of all deaths and was one reason it was reserved for the death of heretics and martyrs who were often one and the same. However, in the context of this section it is necessary to confine the comments to the voluntary burning of the living or self-immolation. It is an interesting fact that throughout history there are records of certain individuals who have voluntarily chosen death by self-immolation. Just a brief list will quickly alert the reader to the fact that these people were diabolically evil or quite mad: Semiramis, queen of Babylon—she married a horse!; Zimri, assassin of Israel (1 Kings 16:18); Heracles [Hercules], Greek demi god; Empedocles, mad Sicilian philosopher; Ashurbanipal, last and cruel king of Assyria; Peregrinus, Greek cynic, and others.[5,6] From the seventeenth to the nineteenth century the Old Believers of Russia, quite sincere but unbalanced Christians, were convinced that the rule of the antichrist was at hand. Starting in 1666 and encouraged by their priests, they went on veritable orgies of self-destruction where hundreds, even entire villages, burned themselves to death.[7] We might recall the Jim Jones affair of the twentieth century. It is an interesting fact that religious extremists from the willing Hindu widow in sutteé to the Buddhist monk in protest, have often chosen suicide by burning.[8,9] The practice was even glorified in opera by Richard Wagner who had his heroine, the cow-horned Brünnhilde, immolate herself on her lover's funeral pyre in the final act of his infamous *Götter-dämmerung*.[10] There can be little doubt that all these misguided individuals were serving the god of this world and not the God of heaven and earth.

Scripture has several examples where God used fire from heaven to punish individuals by burning them alive. The following incident took place during the exodus from Egypt:

Leviticus 10:1-5

> Nadab and Abihu, sons of Aaron, offered profane fire before the Lord: So fire went out from the Lord and devoured them, and they died … Moses called Mishael and Elzaphan … so they went and carried them [bodies of Nadad and Abihu] by their tunics out of the camp.

In 1853 Charles Dickens treated his readers to a new horror in his *Bleak House*. A dissolute and drunken old character had been found burned to a cinder yet his clothes had not even been scorched! Dickens had described a phenomenon known today as Spontaneous Human Combustion [SHC]. The sons of Aaron had evidently suffered a similar fate because those important words *"by their tunics"* indicate that the tunics were not burnt yet the fire *"devoured"* the occupants of those tunics. This is typical of those mysterious cases of SHC where the body, or parts of it, are burnt to a cinder indicating a very high temperature while the clothing is not affected. There are several other incidents in Scripture given in Appendix B that suggest this same strange phenomenon had taken place. The disciples seemed to be familiar with some of these accounts and asked Jesus if He wanted them to *"command fire to come down from heaven and consume the Samaritans"* (Luke 9:54). Hundreds of genuine cases of SHC have been reported throughout the past century by Arnold yet there has never been a satisfactory naturalistic explanation.[11]

Turning now to burning of the dead, that is cremation, this was always associated with God's judgment by fire and considered something fearful by the Israelites. It was also a special case of non-burial. But first, most commentators agree that while the Israelites never normally practiced cremation, there was a special case for the burning of plague victims and it is found in the book of Amos:

Amos 6:10

And when a kinsman of the dead, with one who will burn the bodies, picks up the bodies to take them out of the house, he will say to one inside the house, "Are there anymore with you?" And he will say, "Hold your tongue! For we dare not mention the name of the Lord."

The first example of ceremonial cremation in Scripture is found in Genesis chapter 22 and concerned Abraham who obediently followed God's order to kill and cremate his son Isaac. God stopped the test at the last moment and provided a substitute offering. The normal cremation process, that is, burning of the dead by natural fire, did occur in the Old Testament but it was always employed as a posthumous punishment. During entry to the promised land the nation of Israel was condemned by God because Achan had stolen goods from Jericho. The Lord commanded that he and his family should be stoned to death then burned with fire:

Joshua 7:25

Joshua to Achan at the battle of Ai: And Joshua said,"Why have you troubled us? The Lord will trouble you this day." So all Israel stoned him with stones; and they burned them [Achan's family] with fire after they had stoned them with stones.

Posthumous Punishment

Capital punishment among the Jews was always humane and carried out either by stoning or beheading. For the most heinous crimes, however, death was immediately followed either by hanging or burning. Added "punishment" after death is a concept totally foreign to the modern reader and we tend not to see it when read-ing the Scriptures.[12] Two examples concern hanging the dead:

Joshua 10:26

> And afterwards Joshua struck them [five kings] and killed them, and hanged them on five trees; and they were hanging on the trees until evening.

Esther 9:12-13

> ... the ten sons of Haman the son of Hammedatha, the enemy of the Jews, they [the Jews] killed; Then Esther said, "If it please the king, let it be granted to the Jews who are in Shushan to do again tomorrow according to today's decree, and let Haman's ten sons be hanged on the gallows."

The headless bodies were usually hung by the hands. In the case of the Philistine's treatment of King Saul and his three sons, they were beheaded then the bodies nailed to the wall of Bethshan. The ac-count of the treatment of Saul's body is given in 1 Samuel chapter 31. In the final verses the valiant men of Jabesh Gilead removed the bodies, burned them, buried the bones at Jabesh and fasted seven days to remove their defilement caused by touching the dead.

Commentaries are divided on the reason for burning Saul's body; some even claim it was done in gratitude! At first reading it is natural to conclude that the men of Jabesh Gilead were grateful to Saul for rescuing them from the Ammonites some years earlier. The account is given in 1 Samuel chapter 11, however, it is neces-sary to read 2 Samuel chapter 21 to find the reason for burning. The Gibeonites had deceived Joshua over four centuries earlier but Joshua had agreed to let them live peaceably as hewers of wood and drawers of water for the Israelites (Joshua chapter 9). Saul and his bloodthirsty house were desperately seeking favor with the Lord, had recalled half the story concerning the Gibeonites—the deception but not the promise—and had recently killed many of the Gibeonites. The Gibeonites were thus set upon revenge and al-though the Philistines had killed Saul, they took his body and cre-mated it as a posthumous punishment. Saul's affair caused a famine in the land for three years until David came to make mat-ters right with the Gibeonites (2 Samuel 21:1).

Burning after stoning was reserved for cases of aggravated sin, usually sexual sins.

Deuteronomy 22:21

> ... then they shall bring out the young woman to the door of her father's house, and the men of the city shall stone her to death with stones, because she has done a disgraceful thing in Israel, to play the harlot in her father's house; so you shall put away the evil person from among you.

However, if the father was a priest, the crime was perceived to be more serious and the victim would be stoned as directed above, then the body burned with fire:

Leviticus 21:9

> The daughter of any priest, if she profane herself by playing the harlot, she profanes her father. She shall be burned with fire.

Precisely this situation was first reported when Judah, acting as priest, threatened to stone and burn his widowed daughter-in-law, Tamar (Genesis 38:24). Another instance was for the sin of incest and the case is cited when a man marries a woman and her mother (Leviticus 20:14). All authorities agree however, that the Jews never burned a person alive and never burned a dead body unless it was a plague victim or intended as a punishment. When a criminal was either stoned or beheaded the body was buried. However, when the body was subsequently burned to ashes these were not buried but would either be deliberately scattered or left for the elements to scatter. In other words, burning after death ensured that the body was not buried and, as we have seen before, non-burial defiles the land. In the same way, the burnt bones of those who had been buried in tombs, not in the earth, defiled the pagan altar:

2 Kings 23:16

> And he [Josiah] sent and took the bones out of the tombs and burned them on the altar, and defiled it according to the word of the Lord ...

The Consequences of Defiling the Land

Throughout the Old Testament there are several references to famine. There were famines on two occasions in Canaan at the time of Abram (Genesis 12:10 and 26:1), seven years of famine "over all the world" when Jacob and his sons had to go to Egypt (Genesis 41:53ff) and the famine in Israel but not Moab at the time of Ruth (1:1). At the time of famine these people had to leave their own country to find food and God gave us the reason when He spoke to Moses:

Leviticus 18:25
> God to Moses:
> "For the land is defiled: therefore I visit the punishment of its iniquity upon it, and the land vomits out its inhabitants."

God's justice is not rough justice but is seemingly weighed and measured very precisely with retribution made in exact accordance with the corporate sin. In Genesis 9:6, immediately following the Genesis Flood, God gave man permission to take the life of a murderer in order to administer justice. This was the beginning of human government. Such government may have been godly at first but history shows a dismal record, especially during the past century. The following verse is a glimpse of God's judical system. Here He even knows in advance precisely how much iniquity it will take to defile the land to the point where retribution is necessary:

Genesis 15:16
> [God to Abram] "But in the fourth generation they shall return here, for the iniquity of the Amorites is not yet complete."

Mark 4:24
> And He [Jesus] said to them, "Take heed what you hear, with the same measure you use, it will be measured to you; and to you who hear, more will be given."

Similar sentiments are found in Matthew 7:2 and Luke 6:38. God weighs the iniquity of a nation and when it has come to full measure with the land completely defiled, punishment follows often in the form of famine. Some have argued for and some against the view that the punishment applies to the victim posthumously. The early Church Father, Tertullian, believed that the soul separated from the body about the third day and argued that non-burial of the dead or actual mutilation of the dead, would not cause injury to the soul. However, he added that if injury did occur to the soul by non-burial, then this would be in the highest degree unfair because all the fault lies with the nearest relatives.[13] The responsibility for defilement of the land is indeed that of those who dispose of the dead. Burning of the dead ensures complete non-burial and is the supreme act of disobedience to the commandment that we return to the dust of the ground. Scattering of the ashes adds defiance to disobedience. When the land is completely defiled the punishment is therefore not so much for the victims but rather corporately for the survivors, that is, the nation. One can only wonder if time is not running out for us in the West who for almost two centuries have, at no little expense, dedicatedly practiced non-burial by every means possible.

This concludes the issue of cremation but as it was pointed out in the Preface, cremation is just one of the methods employed by the Father of Lies to destroy the belief in the resurrection. This is by far the more important issue and the following four chapters are included for those readers interested in knowing where church doctrines concerning the origin and destiny of the spirit and the soul come from and why. For others, concerned only with the question of whether it is right for a Christian to be cremated, they are invited to take the direct flight to Chapters 11 and 12 where they will find some very practical advice on preparation for departure.

7

Bias and Understanding Scripture

There are four classes of idols which beset men's minds.
To these for distinction's sake I have assigned names, calling
the first class Idols of the Tribe; the second, Idols of the Cave;
the third, Idols of the Market-Place; the fourth, Idols of the Theatre.

FRANCIS BACON, *NOVUM ORGANUM*. 1620

Why Are There Different Interpretations?

The topic for this book is cremation and, as we have seen, this has led to the broader issue of the attack on the belief in the resurrection. However, along the way we have to address the question of the destiny of the soul. This subject lies beyond the purview of science but our Creator has left us with Scripture as our only source of knowledge. It is here that we are given an understanding of the soul's origin and destiny. To be sure, the Author has seemingly presented the matter in a somewhat arcane fashion and, even when puzzled out, we are still left with many questions. An attempt will be made in the next chapter to set out in a logical order what Scripture tells us about the soul and the spirit. Before doing so, however, we need to address two facts in this present chapter.

In the first place, and with respect, most Christians would probably agree that it would help a great deal if the Scriptures had been given to us in a totally logical manner and without ambiguity. The second fact, directly related to the first, is that every Christian eventually develops a bias in his understanding of Scripture. The result is that Christians are splintered into many Church denominations.

England's Lord Chancellor, Francis Bacon, was speaking about bias or prejudice when he spoke of "idols" in the quote above and church denominations come nicely under the heads "market-place" and "theatre" in Bacon's definition. We know that God is sovereign but to the rational mind it would seem that Christianity might be a greater force if we could all combine into one super-church. The World Council of Churches has this as a principal objective. However, the attempt to produce one super-church happened before at the Tower of Babel and, for our own good, God divided mankind by language, then by color and by religion. The same thing happened again in the early Christian era where, for the first fifteen-hundred years, a hierarchical mega-church became steadily more corrupt. The founding fathers of America were keenly aware of the dangers of the hierarcical church system and knew the safety of small autonomous church congregations.

The following verses are some examples of passages that many might agree Christendom would have been better served had they never been part of Scripture:

1 Samuel 28:10-20.
> Saul's consultation with the witch of En Dor. This is used by those wishing to justify the practice of spiritualism or contacting the dead.

2 Samuel 1:26.
> David to Jonathan: *"Your love to me was wonderful, surpassing the love of women."* An unfortunate verse used to justify homosexuality.

1 Corinthians 15:29.
> Paul's rhetorical statement about *"they who are baptized for the dead"* is a key verse for the Mormon faith and has spawned an "industry" of recording genealogies.

Matthew 17:11-13.
> Here Jesus said to His disciples *"Elijah has come already"* and they understood that He spoke to them of John the Baptist. Believers in reincarnation love this passage.

There are other controversial verses that have caused division within Christendom and, without wishing to further that division, just one will be given. This is that well known verse where Jesus Himself appears to make Peter the first pope:

Matthew 16:18.
> "... and on this rock [*petros*] I will build My church."

Historically, passages such as these have caused a great deal of bloodshed between Catholic and Protestant in the wars of old Europe yet, we have to admit, they are all part of inspired Scripture. In His wisdom God has given us words that have permitted division yet by those same words He has offered us His truth. It is suggested that the clue to this seeming dilemma is to be found in the account of the departure of Elijah, first in 2 Kings 2:1 then 2 Kings 10-11:

2 Kings 2:10-11.

> Elisha had asked for a double portion of Elijah's spirit: "You have asked a hard thing. Nevertheless, if you see me when I am taken from you, it shall be so for you; but if not, it shall not be so." Then it happened, as they continued on and talked, that suddenly a chariot of fire appeared with horses of fire, and separated the two of them; and Elijah went up by a whirlwind into heaven.

In spite of the old Negro spiritual, Elijah did not go to heaven in a chariot but in a whirlwind. Elisha had kept his eyes on Elijah all the while and inherited the double portion. The chariot was only a distraction to test Elisha and this is seemingly the purpose of many of those troublesome verses. God seems to be saying, "Keep your eyes on My Word." By taking the time to do this we will not be distracted by OBE's, Church traditions and popular teachings. If it is acknowledged that man has a free will, no matter how little, then there must be some provision for us to make a choice. There is seldom proof for the things of this world; proof violates choice. We learn to draw our conclusions from evidences, in this case Scripture passages. Even then we cannot expect all passages to be positive, some will be neutral. The choices we make depend upon the willingness to believe and this will eventually determine our bias. Those passages describing posthumous punishment, for example, may have been read dozens of times yet not "seen" by many readers simply because it is completely foreign to our modern way of thinking.

As an illustration using another subject, if our willingness is to believe the theory of evolution, then we shall see what appear to be abundant evidences to support it. However, those "evidences" disappear in the light of better science. On the other hand, if we have the will to believe in the Genesis account of Creation, evidences for Creation will become obvious once pointed out. Moreover, those evidences do withstand inquiry yet, throughout, we may never finish with absolute proof. God will not violate the free will of those unwilling to believe Him; they must be left with something. The same principle seems to apply in the case of Scripture and we are even told about this:

2 Thessalonians 2:10-12.

... among those who perish, because they did not receive the love of the truth, that they might be saved. And for this reason God will send them strong delusion, that they should believe the lie that they all may be condemned who did not believe the truth but had pleasure in unrighteousness.

No matter who we are, and this includes the Bible translators, we have been given a choice to believe the lie or, with a little more diligence, pursue God's truth. Usually indoctrination precedes study and we all finish having a bias towards one interpretation or another. That bias is perpetuated in our system of Christian education today. In North America, seminaries and Bible Colleges are known by the particular dogma they teach, thus from the very first day the student hears the interpretation he has chosen to study. Basically, he will chose from the Augustinian, the Calvinist or the Arminian position. Teaching is done from a Bible translation that supports this same dogma and thus by the time he graduates the student is entirely polarized towards one interpretation. It will only be with difficulty that he will ever see another point of view. Those who have converted from say, the Roman Catholic position to an evangelical Protestant position, will understand perfectly that this has taken time and personal study. Reading the Scriptures in their original languages helps to avoid the translator's theological bias but unfortunately this is beyond the ability of most Christians today.

The next three chapters are based entirely upon Scripture while the intention is to present the Scriptural teaching on the origin and destiny of the soul as logically as possible.

8

The Origin & Destiny of the Soul

Life is real! Life is earnest!
And the grave is not its goal;
"Dust thou art, to dust returnest,"
Was not spoken of the soul.

H.W. LONGFELLOW. *A PSALM OF LIFE* 1838

The Family of Man

Scripture teaches that the whole human race descended from a single mating pair. Paul's Mars Hill address contains these words:

Acts 17:26

> And He has made from one blood every nation
> of men to dwell on all the face of the earth,
> and has determined their pre-appointed times
> and boundaries of their habitation.

There was a time when science told us that man had multiple origins. However, mounting DNA evidence now indicates that we are all related no matter what color we are. This means that all of mankind today has descended from one mating pair. The Bible calls them Adam and Eve and they lived for a while in the Garden of Eden.

Readers will understand that we have a soul and we have a spirit but a major division of opinions begins right at this point. The difficulty is that on a few occasions Scripture appears to use the words "soul" and "spirit" interchangeably. Some therefore believe that the soul and the spirit are one and the same thing, thus man consists of two parts: the body and the soul/spirit. Subscribers to this view are called dichotomists. Others, take the trichotomist view that the soul and the spirit are separate entities, thus man consists of three parts: the body, the soul and the spirit. More will be said about these two positions later but first, we need to see what Scripture says about the origin of the spirit and the soul.

The Origin of the Spirit

The spirit, sometimes translated "wind" or "breath," is taken from the Hebrew word, *ruach,* or its Greek equivalent, *pneuma.* In the moment when God breathed into the image of Adam, He gave Adam both a spirit and a soul although this is not made perfectly clear. Most translations then speak of Adam as a "living soul" meaning that the soul within the body has been given life by the spirit. From God's perspective man is a soul temporarily clothed in a material body and given mortal life. Many commentators believe that God sends His spirit to animate or energize every living thing, including human beings. This is not the Holy Spirit but the spirit of life on loan to each living thing at conception and returned at death. Jesus returned His spirit at death. Psalm 104 seems to express this understanding and there are other verses given in Appendix B that express the same idea:

Psalm 104:29-30

> Referring to the animals:
> You take away their breath [*ruach*],
> they die and return to their dust.
> You send forth Your spirit [*ruach*], they are created
> and You renew the face of the earth.

The Origin of the Soul

The Hebrew word *nephesh* is found over seven-hundred times. In about four-hundred of these occasions it has been translated as "soul," about one-hundred times as "life" and in lesser numbers as "person," "mind," etc. All refer to the person. The Greek equivalent word is *psuche.* It is significant that throughout Scripture neither *nephesh* nor *psuche* ever has any qualifying words such as, "endless," "ever-lasting," or "undying," or any other modifier of equivalent meaning, including "immortal," attached to them. There have been two theories commonly taught to explain the origin of the soul:

The Creation Theory

According to this view God creates a soul for each body and this enters the individual immediately upon conception. This theory is said to explain how an immortal soul can occupy a mortal body but the immortality of the soul is assumed in the first place. There are five Scriptures cited to support the view that God is the immediate creator of every soul. These are listed below but it will be seen that most of these verses refer to the spirit rather than the soul. Here the dichotomist permits the word "spirit" to be read as "soul." We find that the dichotomist position and the Creation Theory are very popular in North America but there are more than just a few difficulties:

Numbers 16:22
> O God, the God of the spirits [*ruach*] of all flesh.

Ecclesiastes 12:7
> [At death] … and the spirit will return to God who gave it.

Isaiah 57:16
> For the spirit [*ruach*] would fail before Me,
> And the souls [*nephesh*] which I have made.

Zechariah 12:1
> … the Lord who… lays the foundation of the earth,
> and forms the spirit [*ruach*] of man within him.

Hebrews 12:9
> … be in subjection to the Father of spirits [*pneuma*] and live.

One problem with this theory is related to the transfer of human personality from parent to child but of more importance are the Scriptural difficulties. Genesis 2:1-3 teaches that God finished His work of creation on the sixth day. Therefore to suppose that He is still busy creating souls by the hour and minute would appear to be contrary to Scripture. There is also the grave objection that since the Scriptures are very clear about the sinfulness of man's soul, then as Creator of each individual soul, God becomes the author of sin. To avoid this, the Creationist argues that while each soul is created in purity it becomes sinful upon introduction to the human body. Another serious objection to this theory is that it sows the seeds of dualism by positing separate origins for the soul and the body and thus makes separate destinies easier to accept. In short, this theory supports neo-platonism.

The Traducian Theory

This theory holds that the entire human race has derived from Adam and that during the propagation process both the material and immaterial nature of man are transferred. In this case, God is the mediate creator of the human soul, that is, He created only the first and pure soul given to Adam. Subsequently, the whole of mankind has inherited Adam's fallen nature. There are a number of verses commonly cited in support of the Traducian Theory and two are given below:

Job 15:14
> What is man that he could be pure? And he that is born of woman, that he could be righteous?

Ephesians 2:3
> Paul: Among whom also we all once conducted ourselves in the lusts of the flesh, ... and were by nature children of wrath, just as the others.

Two other, rather picturesque passages, tell the reader that the souls—the *nephesh*—of succeeding generations reside in the loins of the first. Clearly, if the *nephesh*, are in the loins, God does not have to produce them to order as required by the Creation Theory. These two verses are given below in both the KJV and NKJV translations to illustrate translator bias:

Genesis 46:26
> KJV: All the souls [*nephesh*] that came with Jacob into Egypt, who came out of his loins ...
>
> NKJV: All the persons who went with Jacob to Egypt, who came from his body ...

Exodus 1:5
> KJV: And all the souls [*nephesh*] that came out of the loins of Jacob, were seventy souls ...
>
> NKJV: All those who were descendants of Jacob were seventy persons

The words "persons" and "descendants" instead of "souls" in the NKJV version strongly indicates that the translator was biased towards the Creation Theory for the origin of the soul.

Both Augustine and later Luther, were undecided about these theories and to this day theologians are still undecided. However, as far as has been briefly set out here, the Traducian Theory would appear to best be in accord with Scripture and explain our participation in Adam's sin.

———o◯o———

Christian Doctrines on the Destiny of the Soul

There are two schools of teaching regarding the destiny of the soul:

1. The major school is based upon neo-platonism i.e. the belief that the soul is innately immortal and separates from the body at death. This school is in turn divided into dichotomists and trichotomists: The dichotomists are likely the more numerous and argue that man consists of two parts, that is, the body and the soul/spirit. The trichotomists argue that man is divided into three parts, that is, the body, the soul and the spirit.

2. The minor school rejects neo-platonism, believes that man is trichotomous and teaches that the soul is conditionally immortal and does not separate from the body at death. First, we need to see where the dichotomous and trichotomous arguments come from and why.

Dichotomous Man

John Calvin (1509–1564) was a highly educated young lawyer raised in a Catholic family and "converted" at the age of 24. Just one year later he had produced a work with the awful title *Psychopannychia*. In this he claimed that the soul was a substance and that it continued to live after the body dies.[1] Two years later he began to publish his more famous *Institutes of the Christian Religion* and here he fully sets out the dichotomous position:

> "... *man consists of body and a soul; meaning by soul, an immortal though created essence ... sometimes he is called a spirit. But though the two terms, while they are used together, differ in their meaning, still when this is used by itself it* [the spirit] *is equivalent to the soul, as when Solomon speaking of death says, 'the spirit returns to God who gave it'.*"[2]

Calvin had been taught Augustine's view and thus accepted neo-platonic teaching on the soul early in his education. It was this teaching and a few verses that caused Calvin to assume that the soul and the spirit were essentially the same thing. While on most occasions in Scripture the use of the words "soul" and "spirit" is reasonably straightforward, it must be admitted that on a few occasions *psuche* and *pneuma* are seemingly used interchangeably in the original Greek. Commentators are uncertain of the reason and we might wonder if it is related to that freewill choice. An example of this interchangeability by the same author [John] and only a few verses apart indicate that both the *psuche* and the *pneuma* can be "troubled:"

John 12:27

> Jesus speaking: Now my soul [*psuche*] is troubled ...

John 13:21

> Jesus: He was troubled in spirit [*pneuma*].

Calvin took the position that the soul and the spirit were one and the same thing. His reference to Solomon from his *Institutes'* in the quote above, is taken from the Book of Eccesiastes where the spirit now becomes the soul/spirit who returns to God:

Ecclesiastes 12:7

> [Upon death] ... and the spirit will return to God who gave it.

This verse has well-served since to get the expired Christian immediately into heaven. Calvin had adopted the dichotomous position within a year or so of being converted and these first works, written in youthful enthusiasm, did not suggest but proclaimed that man was dichotomous. It would not be an entirely honest statement to say that the dichotomous view defines the characteristics of the soul/spirit clearly. The reader may recall the adult Sunday school class with the blackboard diagram of intersecting circles. Like the peace of God, it seems to pass all understanding! Nevertheless, this is the usual teaching on the soul offered in mainline Protestant Churches throughout North America today. Its source is John Calvin.

Trichotomous Man

This is the oldest position and is more common today in the Eastern Churches than in North America. Little reference is made to those few cases of interchangeability and man is simply a three-part being with specific characteristics ascribed to each part. Essentially the soul is the person and the spirit provides the life. The principal Scripture supporting the trichotomous position occurs in the account of the creation of Adam:

Genesis 2:7

> And the Lord God formed man of the dust of the ground, and breathed into his nostrils the breath [*neshamah*] of life [*chaiyim*]; and man became a living being.

Genesis 2:17
> God: "...in the day that you eat of it you shall surely die."

Here the Hebrew text for life is plural [*chaiyim* = lives]. God's breath [*neshamah* not *ruach*] produced two lives: life for the body and life for the soul. When Adam Fell he lost the life of his soul and in God's view he "died" on that day. Jesus spoke of letting *"the dead bury their own dead"* (Matthew 8:22) but Christ gives our souls life once more by His Holy Spirit. Paul makes the situation clearer when he speaks of the body, soul and spirit as three distinct parts of man's nature in his farewell to the Thessalonians and a distinction also appears in the book of Hebrews:

1 Thessalonians 5:23
> Now may the God of peace Himself sanctify you completely; and may your whole spirit [*ruach*], soul [*psuche*], and body [*soma*] be preserved blameless at the coming of our Lord Jesus.

Hebrews 4:12
> For the word of God is ... sharper than any two-edged sword, piercing even to the division of soul [*psuche*] and spirit [*ruach*], and of joints and marrow.

Although Scripture does not clearly say that man is a three-part being it does seem to be strongly implied. Moreover, it is accepted by all Christians that God is triune and since man is made in God's image and likeness, the balance of judgment would seem to weigh in favour of man being trichotomous. Heibert has put the matter this way: *"Students of Scripture are not agreed as to whether the distinction between spirit and soul ... is substantial or functional. Trichotomists hold to the former, dichotomists to the latter."* [3]

The Innately Immortal Soul

While theories on the origin of the soul or the division of man may not seem like very serious issues, whichever view is adopted can, in the long run, effectively support or deny the belief in the general resurrection. We saw above that the Creation Theory for the origin of the soul introduces dualism that directly supports the separation of the soul from the body. In a similar way, the teaching of dichotomous man also supports the immediate separation of the soul/spirit from the body. It has been stated repeatedly that the original promise of immortality offered in the Garden was introduced to the Jews at about the time of Christ then introduced into the Christian Church less than two centuries later. Today, the words "immortal soul" drift mindlessly from a thousand pulpits of evangelical churches without a whimper of protest from Bereans asleep in their pews. It was stated earlier and bears repeating again that neither in the Old Testament nor in the New do the Hebrew and Greek words translated "soul" have any qualifying words to indicate that the soul is immortal. We also saw in Chapter Four that the doctrine of neo-platonism, that is, the innately immortal soul, has been sustained throughout the centuries by OBE's and other methods including the introduction of the practice of cremation. All these tactics ultimately destroy belief in the general resurrection.

The argument for the immortal soul is almost circular in that it begins with the assumption that the soul is innately immortal then Scriptures are found that appear to support it and this is then offered as evidence that the soul is, in fact, immortal. Immortality will apply to both saint and sinner and in each case, since the conscious soul cannot accompany the body to the grave, it must depart upon death. For the Protestant there are only two alternative destinations: the Christian goes to heaven and the sinner goes to hell. The sinner, like Prometheus, is immortal and indestructible and suffers for all eternity. This is essentially what is taught in most North American Protestant churches. Generally unstated is the fact that the rewards for both saint and sinner, that is, paradise or punishment, are received before the resurrection and before the judgment. In a very real sense this makes the resurrection and judgment redundant. According to Scripture the judgment follows the resurrection.

Matthew 16:27

> For the Son of Man will come in the glory of His Father with His Angels, and then He will reward each according to his works.

Hebrews 9:27

> And it is appointed for men to die once, but after this the judgment.

The neo-platonic teaching that the Christians will have direct entry to heaven also has other problems: Scripture speaks of a glorified body received at the resurrection but nowhere does it speak of an interim body for the time we are in heaven waiting for the resurrection.

Two passages, the first from Jesus and the second from Paul should place the immortality of the soul into question:

Matthew 10:28
> And do not fear those who kill the body but cannot kill the soul, [*psuche*] but rather fear Him [God] who is able to destroy both soul and body in hell [*gehenna*].

1 Timothy 6:15-16
> King of kings and Lord of lords who **alone** has immortality

No matter what definition is applied to the soul [*psuche*], immortality [*athanasia*] is the one quality that cannot be included according to this verse.

The Conditionally Immortal Soul

The doctrine of Conditional immortality rejects neo-platonic teaching, accepts the greater Scriptural evidence rather than the exceptions and adopts the trichotomous position. The Conditionalist teaching was that of the early Church and has existed as a minority view throughout the centuries. However, it may be new to many readers and the whole of Chapter Ten has been given to its description.

Today, while most laymen do not actually deny the resurrection, many are somewhat confused about the teaching they have received. We saw in Chapter Two that among the Church hierarchy, particularly of the Church of England, we find some rank unbelief in the Resurrection of Christ. It goes without saying that the general resurrection of man will eventually fall by the wayside. Fortunately, not all Christians subscribe to these teachings.

In the next chapter we will take a closer look at those familiar passages usually quoted in defense of the immortal and separable soul.

9

But What Do the Scriptures Say?

There is a land of pure delight
Where saints immortal reign;
Infinite day excludes the night,
And pleasures banish pain.

ISAAC WATTS, *HYMNS* ... 2: 65.

In the previous chapter we saw that there are two schools of teaching about the destiny of the soul. The major teaching is neo-platonic and assumes that man consists of either two parts or three parts and that the soul/spirit or the soul is innately immortal and separable. The minor teaching rejects neo-platonism, believes man consists of three parts and that the soul is conditionally immortal and does not separate until the day of resurrection. In this chapter we will briefly examine the principal Scriptures rehearsed in Bible commentaries and footnotes to defend the neo-platonic view. The Conditionalist teaching will be given in Chapter Ten. Below is a brief recapitulation of the definition of the key words:

HEBREW	GREEK	ENGLISH
Nephesh	*Psuche*	Soul, life, mind, the person
Ruach	*Pneuma*	Spirit, wind, breath

Texts Used to Teach Innate Immortality
The Death of Rachel

Genesis 35:18

> And so it was, as her soul [*nephesh*] was departing,
> (for she died), that she called his name Ben-Oni;
> but his father called him Benjamin.

Rachael died in child-birth. Massive hemorrhaging is the cause of death in childbirth and her *nephesh* [soul] was departing from her body and, quite properly, returning to the dust of the ground via her blood. We have here a parallel case with modern embalming where the soul is flushed out of the body with the blood. This passage does not support the immortal soul but is rather a special case of the separation of the soul. Further, we are not told that her soul was going to *sheol* [the grave] or to paradise [heaven] so that the passage is neutral in its support of either the innately immortal soul or the conditionally immortal soul positions.

The Witch of En Dor

1 Samuel 28:7-19
> Then the woman said, "Whom shall I bring up for you?" And he [Saul] said, "Bring up Samuel for me." ... And she said, "An old man is coming up, and he is covered with a mantle." ... Now Samuel said to Saul, "Why have you disturbed me by bringing me up?"

In this account the prophet Samuel had been dead some two years and buried at Ramah and King Saul badly needed advice. Although forbidden to do so according Deuteronomy 18:10-12 and the laws of the land, Saul consulted the witch or medium and, by her black arts, she purportedly raised the soul of Samuel. This account may sometimes be used to support the separable soul position but more importantly it is used as a Biblical precedent by those who practice spiritualism. The first question may be, is it actually possible to contact the dead? For the curious an account will be found in Homer's *Odyssey*. The fact that Scripture forbids the practice suggests that some sort of spirit contact is possible. Most commentators think that the probable explanation is that the witch contacted a familiar or impersonating evil spirit rather than the soul of Samuel. First Chronicles 10:13-14 in the NKJV tells us that the reason Saul was killed in battle was because *"he consulted a medium for guidance."* The KJV translates this as *"asking counsel of one who has a familiar spirit"* but it has to be admitted that this passage does not make it absolutely clear that it was a familiar spirit. Ecclesiastes 9:5-10 tells us that, *"the dead know nothing"* and, *"there is no knowledge or wisdom in the grave"* so that from just these two verses it would seem highly unlikely that it was Samuel. Nevertheless, since what the spirit said proved to be correct it does leave the question: Is Scripture trying to teach us something from this account? This is one of those passages where there is insufficient conclusive evidence to support either the separable and conscious soul or the unconscious sleeping soul position. However, the Conditionalist school does not use the account of the witch of En Dor to support the argument that the witch had awakened a sleeping soul.

Elijah Raises a Dead Child

1 Kings 17:21-22

> And he [Elijah] stretched himself out on the child three times, and cried out to the Lord and said, "O Lord my God, I pray let this child's soul [nephesh] come back to him."

This case would certainly seem to suggest the separation of the soul from the body while the following verse (22) states that the soul, not the spirit, came back. In this case, we are not told that the child had bled to death nor are we told that the spirit had left but we can conclude that his soul had left. Further than that there is simply insufficient information to conclude from this passage whether the child's soul was in paradise, in sheol or just a few feet away?

Upon Old Age and Death

Ecclesiastes 12:6-7

> Remember your creator before the silver cord is loosed ... then the dust will return to the earth as it was, and the spirit [ruach] will return to God who gave it.

Here it is the ruach [spirit] that returns to God, not the nephesh [soul]. The dichotomist argues from this passage that while the author wrote "spirit" what was really meant was "soul/spirit." The trichotomist does not use this verse to claim the immortality of the soul.

Soul Departs on the Third Day

Hosea 6:2

> After two days He will revive us: On the third day He will raise us up, that we may live in His sight.

While this passage is not used to teach the separable immortal soul among Christians, it was very important to those Hellenic Jews who lost their belief in the resurrection. They interpreted the passage to support the view that following death the soul remained in the body or very close to it and departed for *sheol* on the third day. Here the meaning of *sheol* changed slightly from referring to the grave to meaning a collective place of retribution for the conscious dead. This made the future resurrection redundant. The idea is more persistant than may be imagined not only among Christians, Jews and Muslims but was found even in the most remote tribes by early missionaries. Among Western Christians, for example, our three-day wake is simply a tradition added to by fears of premature burial. The Muslims believe the soul lingers in the grave for forty days before departure and in the far East protect the buried soul from the heat of the sun with a parasol over the new grave. In order to thoroughly refute the third-day idea and establish the truth of the future resurrection, Jesus deliberated waited four days, not three, before raising Lazarus. To this day, not even believers in the immortal soul will argue that Lazarus' soul had left his body during those four days. Robert Browning's *Epistle of Karshish* claims to recount what Lazarus did and saw during those days but this is purely a fictional writing. Finally, certain theologians in the nineteenth century used this Hosea passage to argue that this was a prophetic statement referring to Christ's resurrection on the third day. It was controversial at the time and few scholars would subscribe to it today.

Moses and Elijah at the Transfiguration

Matthew 17:1-9
> Jesus commanded them, saying, "Tell the vision to no one until the Son of Man is risen from the dead." (v.9)

Often when this passage is used the quote stops at verse eight. Verse nine is the key to understanding that the transfiguration experience was a vision. The passage does not say that it was the souls of Moses and Elijah that were speaking to Jesus and it could not be Moses and Elijah in their glorified resurrected bodies because Jesus was the firstborn from the dead (Revelation 1:5). The usual interpretation is that the figures of Moses and Elijah appeared to represent the fact that the law (Moses) and the prophets (Elijah) had been fulfilled in Christ.

The Parable of the Rich Man and Lazarus. Luke 16:14-31

This passage is only found in the gospel of Luke, the Greek physician, and is the chief cornerstone supporting the separation of the soul after death and the endless torment for the wicked. It is usually claimed not to be a parable but an actual teaching by Christ Himself on the destiny of the soul. However, many Bible translations e.g. the NKJV, refer to it by their subject headings as a parable while in the overall context it is found to be the fifteenth parable in a total of twenty-seven. Some commentators have made the point that this parable comes as the climax to three previous parables: The lost sheep (15:1-7), the lost coin (15:8-10) and the lost (prodigal) son (15:11-32). The parable of the rich man is that of the lost opportunity. Jesus began many of His Lucian parables in the same way: "*A certain man gave a great supper ...*" (14:16) and "*A certain man had two sons ...*" (15:11), etc. and the rich man and Lazarus begins the same way.

In its overall context this passage is of Jesus addressing the Pharisees (v.14) and specifically it concerns bending of the marriage laws (v.18). Jesus then provides this parable in which the rich man represents those who have all the wisdom, that is, the riches of the Law. These rulers keep the law to themselves and dispense perceived exceptions and loopholes at great cost only to those who can afford it. Precisely this same situation has prevailed over the same issue in the Roman church concerning annulment of the first marriage to permit a second.

Further, if this Lucian passage is actually a teaching that the souls of the wicked go to a place of endless torment immediately after death, then the torment takes place before the resurrection and before the judgment. Reasonably, Jesus would not teach something that was not Scriptural. However, the situation is easily resolved when it is shown to be a parable to expose the false teaching then current among the Pharisees. Jewish historian Josephus, writing at about the time of Christ, describes the Greek teaching on hades.[1] The Pharisees teaching was precisely that of the Greeks and as given in the parable told by Jesus; they even used the same expressions "Abraham's bosom" and "Paradise." The Pharisees had adopted the Platonic teaching of the immortal soul with immediate separation followed by paradise and eternal torment for the righteous and the wicked respectively. Jesus turned this false teaching around to make it a parable to teach that eternal destiny is decided in this present life and that there is no second probation.

It is sometimes argued that this passage in Luke cannot be a parable since it contains a proper noun, that is, the name Lazarus. However, this was undoubtedly a deliberate inclusion because later, a man of that very name was resuscitated, not resurrected, from the dead (John chap. 11). By actually raising Lazarus, Jesus proclaimed to the unbelieving Hellenized Jews that on the last day the dead will be raised. Faced with the fact of resucitaion from the truly dead, this gave no choice for belief and caused both Saducees and Pharisees to finally take action and destroy the evidence. They succeeded in the case of Jesus and made the attempt in the case of Lazarus (John 12:10).

Not God of the Dead but the Living

Luke 20:35-38

> [Jesus] "But those who are counted worthy to attain that age, and the resurrection from the dead, neither marry nor are given in marriage; nor can they die anymore, for they are equal to the angels and are sons of God, being sons of the resurrection. Now even Moses showed in the burning bush passage that the dead are raised, when he called the Lord 'the God of Abraham, the God of Isaac, and the God of Jacob.' For He [God] is not the God of the dead but of the living, for all live to Him."

This passage is used to show that while Abraham, Isaac and Jacob died physically they are still alive as souls and God is their Lord. The immortal soul position assumes that their souls are fully conscious and thus in heaven but the verse does not state this. This is another of those neutral passages where there is insufficient information to draw this conclusion. In fact, the souls of Abraham, Isaac and Jacob could equally as well be in an unconscious state or sleeping like the planted seed, waiting for the resurrection day.

Jesus and the Repentant Thief

Luke 23:39-43

> Assuredly, I say to you, today you will be with Me in paradise.... Father, into Your hands I commend My spirit [*pneuma*].

This is a popular passage to claim the immediacy-in-heaven message for the immortal soul. When Jesus made his promise to the repentant thief he did not, would not, lie in His dying moments. Yet, according to Scripture, it would be another forty-three days before Jesus Himself entered paradise. Paradise is where the tree of life now is (Revelation 2:7) and thus it is in the heavenly realm and decidedly not in hades. Jesus had not gone to hades nor returned to His Father even on the third day after His crucifixion. Jesus told Mary in the garden: "*Do not cling to Me, for I have not yet ascended to my Father.*" (John 20:17). Further, it was unlikely that the thief could have been in paradise that day either because he was still alive at sundown when the soldiers broke his legs (John 19:31). However, none of these difficulties would arise if Jesus was correct when He said that "*Lazarus sleeps*" and agreed with Martha that he would rise again in the resurrection (John 11:11-14). In this case, the thief would indeed meet with Christ in paradise on that future resurrection day and experience death as "*the twinkling of an eye*," that is, as being the same day as when the promise had been made.

Paul's Lament to be Present with the Lord

2 Corinthians 5:6-9

> ... while we are at home in the body we are absent from the Lord. We are ... well pleased rather to be absent from the body and to be present with he Lord.

This is another popular passage claiming that from the lips of the apostle Paul himself we have the assurance of a separable soul that takes us immediately to heaven. Taking this passage in complete context we must go back to the previous Corinthian chapter where we see that Paul was writing as an older man and spoke about the outward man perishing (4:16). He had endured flogging five times, beaten with rods three times and stoned once (11:24-25); he must have been in bad physical shape and tired of the struggle of life. He had probably come to realize that Christ was not going to return in his lifetime and there was little likelihood that, like Elijah, he would be translated directly to heaven. His wish was therefore to leave this vale of tears and, perhaps not in the way he had hoped, he became a martyr a few short years later. We can be quite certain that he was fully aware of Plato's teachings and the effect that it had had on the beliefs of his fellow Jews. In fact, it was these same Jews who had come to disbelieve in the resurrection who had been responsible for flogging him five times. Paul tells us in his appeal to King Agrippa:

Acts 26:5-8

> "They [the Jews] knew me [Paul] from the first ... I stand
> and am judged for the hope of the promise made by God
> to our fathers. To this promise our twelve tribes earnestly
> serving God night and day, hope to attain. For this hope's
> sake, King Agrippa, I am accused by the Jews. Why should
> it be thought incredible by you that God raises the dead?"

While some Jews did not believe in the resurrection others paid lip-service to it, but throughout, when faced with evidence that God had actually raised one man, Jesus, from the dead, they saw this as blasphemy. The fact is, it was really a refutation of their unbelief and this was the reason the Jews of Jerusalem sought to kill Paul. At issue was the hope in the resurrection.

With this background and from his writings, we can be confident that Paul had not accepted Plato's immortal soul. He knew that he would not leave this earth until the trumpet called him on that resurrection day but he also knew that he would experience the time of death as "*the twinkling of an eye.*" As we shall see in the next chapter, this is perfectly explained by conditional immortality. Thus, when he said he would be "*pleased rather to be absent from the body **and** to be present with the Lord*" this was a double statement. He wanted to be free from a broken body and he wanted to be present with the Lord. The tendendency is to read "is" for "and" and give the statement an immediacy that is implied rather than stated. Finally, if Paul actually meant that he would be immediately in heaven, this raises the difficult question of an interim body for the period in heaven between death and the resurrection. Paul tells us that we shall "*be clothed with our habitation which is from heaven,*" (2 Corinthians 5:2-4), that is, the glorified body but this is given at the resurrection. Scripture says nothing about an interim body.

Appointed for Eternal Life

Acts 13:48

> When the gentiles heard this, they were glad and honored
> the word of the Lord; and all who were appointed for
> eternal life believed.

This passage is sometimes used to support the immortal soul position for Believers by quoting "*appointed for eternal life*" but there are two problems. The first is that the word "appointed" means arranged for a time in the future but the passage is assumed to mean that eternal life is received at the moment of belief. Revelation 22:14 indicates that eternal life is received in future at the tree of life, not at the moment of conversion. The second problem is one of logic. While the passage regarding those who seek eternal life will be given eternal life (Romans 2:7) is indeed true, the converse position must also be true. That is, unbelievers will not be given eternal life. It is then difficult to see how unbelievers can suffer for all eternity without an eternal life in which suffering can be experienced.

Departure or Decease?

While not often used to support the immortal soul position we should, nevertheless, leave no stone unturned and include this argument based upon the Greek word *"exodos."* This appears only three times in the New Testament, means to exit or depart and has been correctly translated as "departure" in some translations. Other translations try to avoid colloquialisms and use the word "decease" or even "death" to make it absolutely clear to the reader.

Luke 9:31

> At the Mount of Transfiguration:
> Moses and Elijah appeared and spoke of His decease
> [*exodos*] which He was about to accomplish at Jerusalem.
> [RSV, NIV, departure; KJV, NKJV, decease]

2 Peter 1:14-15

> [Peter] I must put off my tent, ... ensure that you always
> have a reminder of these things after my decease [*exodos*].
> [RSV, NIV, departure; KJV, NKJV, decease, GOOD NEWS,
> death]

Hebrews 11:22

> By faith Joseph, when he was dying, made mention of the
> departure [*exodos*] of the children of Isreal.
> [RSV, exodus; KJV, departing; NKJV, departure]

While the word "departure" is strictly correct in all three cases, its use in the first two passages quoted above means departure from this life but it can easily lead to the understanding that reference is being made to the departure of the soul from the body. It is in this latter sense that the immortal soul position is justified.

In this chapter we have taken a critical look at those passages of Scripture used to support the neo-platonist position. In truth, there are difficulties: some passages offer no support, others can be interpreted in a quite different way and others are neutral. In the following chapter we will look at those Scripture passages used to support the position of conditional immortality. The reader will then have most of the facts upon which to draw a conclusion about what the Author of Scripture has actually told us about the soul.

10

What is Conditional Immortality?

The idea of death as a state of dormancy ...
Is the most ancient, the most popular,
And the most constant image of the beyond.

PHILIPPE ARIÈS, *THE HOUR OF OUR DEATH*. 1981

Texts Used to Teach Conditional Immortality

Theologians have a fine term for that period between death and the resurrection. It is called the *interim refrigerium* and it has been the subject of endless debate. Those who subscribe to the immortal soul position tend to dismiss this period or perhaps confine it to microseconds since they argue that the separated soul will immediately be in heaven or hell. Conditionalists claim that the soul stays with the body or near it in a deeply unconscious state that Scripture refers to as "sleep;" it is commonly referred to as "soul sleep." The *interim refrigerium* in this case can be any length of time amounting to thousands of years back to Adam. This was the teaching of the very early Church Fathers but beginning in the second century it was gradually replaced by neo-platonism. The Conditionalist position is trichotomist and has been the persistent minority view throughout Church history. World renowned French social historian, Philippe Ariès, makes the following statement regarding the interpretation based upon conditional immortality:

> *"The idea of death as a state of dormancy has resisted centuries of suppression by the literi. It is found in liturgy and funerary art. The idea of sleep is the most ancient, the most popular, and the most constant image of the beyond. Even today it has not yet disappeared, despite competition from other kinds of images."* [1]

The Conditionalist doctrine is found in some surprising places among the denominations of the Christian Church today. Article #40 of the original Articles of Faith issued by the Convocation of the

Church of England in 1553 condemned the doctrine of soul sleep. However, in 1563 some minor adjustments were made and Article #40 was removed leaving the familiar Thirty-Nine Articles. More recently, some deficiencies in the teaching on the destiny of the soul were recognized and in 1962 the line in the Apostles' Creed "*He descended into hell*" was changed to "*He descended to the dead.*" Today, the Anglican Church does not deny soul sleep while many in the evangelical arm of that Church hold to it quite openly. Some Lutherans also believe in soul sleep as might be expected from Martin Luther's position although the Lutheran Church generally regard this as a skeleton in Luther's cupboard. Luther was actually convinced of soul sleep and expressed it this way:

> "*For just as a man who falls asleep and sleeps soundly until morning does not know what has happened to him when he wakes up, so we shall suddenly rise on the Last Day; and we shall not know neither what death has been like or how we have come through it.*" [2]

The Meaning of the Word "Sleep" in Scripture

The Conditionalist teaching is built around the Scripture's use of the word "sleep" where we would normally use the word "dead." Scripture teaches that there are two deaths, the first and the second. From God's viewpoint our physical death is regarded as "sleep" and is the first death. The Christian is promised that he will not see the second death, in fact, salvation means saved from the second death. The second death is reserved for the unrepentant sinner. The words "sleep," "asleep," and "slept" are used 147 times in Scripture and these have been derived from the Hebrew words: *radam, shena, shakab* and *yashen* and the Greek words: *hupnos, katheudo* and *koimaomai*. Of this total, the word "sleep" or its derivatives, has been used to mean physical death in almost half [45%] of these occasions. A summary of the use of the word "sleep" in our English translations and the frequency of meaning is given in Appendix B.

The Hebrew word, *yashen*, means normal sleep but is modified to mean death when used in Psalm 13:3 as the "*sleep of death*" or in Jeremiah 51:57 as "*perpetual sleep.*" The other Hebrew word *shakab* is generally found in the formula "*he slept with his fathers*" meaning he was buried in the family plot. The Greek word *kaimaomai* is used to mean physical death on every occasion except four. As a matter of interest, *koimaomai* is related to the word *koimeterion* meaning a resting place and, with their understanding, the early Christians adopted this and it became the English word "cemetery," or "the sleeping place." Inspection of any old cemetery will show that the epitaphs nearly always speak of "Resting in Peace", or "Sleeping in Jesus." In the majority of cases then, *shakab* and *kaimaomai,* are translated as "sleep" and mean physical death and this is usually clear from the context. The following are examples:

Deuteronomy 31:16

The Lord said to Moses: "Behold, you will rest with your fathers." [*shakab*, NKJV = rest, KJV = sleep]

There are 39 similar passages in the Old Testament where *shakab* ["sleep"] means death and burial in the family plot. More examples are given from the New Testament in Appendix B.

Death is the Departure of the Spirit

Psalm 146:3-4

His spirit [*ruach*] departs, he returns to the earth ...

Ecclesiastes 12:7

Then the dust will return to the earth as it was,
and the spirit [*ruach*] will return to God who gave it.

James 2:26

For as the body without the spirit [*pneuma*] is dead,
so faith without works is dead also.

It is the *ruach* or the *pneuma* [spirit] that departs and goes back to God who gave it. The person, "he," returns to his earth and is a re-minder that Adam was created from the dust of the ground. The Conditionalist argues that the *nephesh* [soul], does not separate but remains unconscious and secure in the place of interment until the general resurrection. This is supported by those passages that claim the righteous dead will hear from the grave:

John 5:25, 28:

[Jesus] Most assuredly I say to you, the hour is coming, and now is, when the dead will hear the voice of the Son of God; and those who hear will live .... Do not marvel at this; for the hour is coming in which all who are in the graves will hear His voice.

1 Thessalonians 4:16

> For the Lord Himself will descend from heaven with a shout, with the voice of an archangel, and with the trumpet of God. And the dead in Christ will rise first [i.e. those who have the Spirit of Christ].

It has been argued that it is the body that will hear the shout but all but a very few bodies will have been dissolved to dust or rotting. The hearing comes in response to the shout and prior to the resurrection of the glorified body. Thus, only the soul and the accompanying Spirit of Christ, are in the grave to respond to the shout.

Our Interim Destiny is the Grave

Before setting out the evidence for this statement we need to meet a popular objection. It is commonly argued from Revelation 6:9-11 that the destiny of the Christian is in heaven, not the grave, because the saints are under the altar. This is a misreading because it is the martyrs who are under the altar, not the saints. However, there is an interesting insight from this passage that is worth mentioning:

Revelation 6:9-11

> When he opened the fifth seal, I saw under the altar the souls of those who had been slain for the word of God and for the testimony which they held. And they cried with a loud voice saying, "How long, O Lord, holy and true, until You judge and avenge our blood on those who dwell on earth?" And a white robe was given to each ...

Very few Christians in our comfortable Western pews will be killed for the Word of God although that day may well come. The giving of the white robes provides more insight. The souls were of those *"slain for the Word of God,"* that is, the martyred Christians of the New Testament and likely the martyred prophets of the Old. White robes can only have been given if those souls had been given bodies to wear them. Knowing that *"flesh and blood cannot inherit the kingdom of God"* (1 Cor. 15:50) those bodies must be glorified bodies, that is, resurrected bodies. Further, their resurrection cannot have taken place before the Resurrection of Christ because Christ is *"the first born from the dead"* (1 Colossians 1:18). The question then arises, why were the souls of the martyrs under the altar if the souls of other Christians remain in the grave or, from the neo-platonist view, if they are enjoying heaven? The history of the Christian Church shows that there has been a veritable industry of praying to the saints, that is, those in the understanding of the Latin and Roman Church, who were martyrs. The business of the witch of En Dor will be recalled and, while this was undoubtedly a familiar spirit, if necromancy is at all possible, Scripture may be telling us something here and the words of the spirit, *"Why have you disturbed me by bringing me up?"* (1 Samuel 28:15) then become significant. The Old Testament speaks of the altar as a place of refuge and we might wonder if the souls of the martyrs and perhaps those notables Enoch, Moses and Elijah reside in sleep under the altar as a place of refuge and protection from necromancers?

There are a number of verses that say that both Believers and non-believers remain in the grave while the reference is to the person, the immaterial part of us who sleeps and wakes. Every material part eventually disappears completely.

Psalm 6:5

> For in death there is no rememberance of You [God];
> in the grave [*sheol*] who will give You [God] thanks?

Daniel 12:2

> And many of those who sleep [*yashen*] in the dust of the
> earth shall awake, some to everlasting life, some to shame
> and ever lasting contempt.

The early Hebrew understanding of the word *sheol* [grave] was the place where the soul goes to after death and was identified with the place of burial. However, under the influence of Greek thinking, *sheol* became a gloomy place of retribution where conscious souls were gathered meaning that the souls had separated from their bodies. Finally, and just before the time of Christ, an entire doctrine had been formed whereby *sheol* was a place divided by a great gulf. On the one side was a pleasant place for the righteous and on the other side, close to *gehenna* [the lake of fire], was an awful place where the wicked awaited their judgment and eventual fate. The Jewish historian, Josephus,[3] in his Dissertation VI has left us with a most detailed account of the Jewish understanding at the time of Christ of *sheol* or rather *hades*, since they were Greek-speaking Jews. The self cannot be conscious no matter where it is or there would be some kind of rememberance (Psalm 6:5). From God's viewpoint, what we understand to be death, He calls "sleep." Jesus answered the Sadduces on their question of the resurrection and told them plainly by quoting Exodus 3:6 that "*God is not the God of the dead but of the living*" meaning that from God's viewpoint Abraham, Isaac and Jacob were still alive (Matthew 22:32). Death is then a deeply unconscious state of the soul but, like the planted seed, it still lives even thousands of years but is experienced as "*the twinkling of an eye.*"

Abel's Blood

Genesis 4:10

> And He [God] said, "What have you done? The voice of your brother's blood cried out to Me from the ground [*adamah*]."

Abel's voice to God could not come from his body while his spirit had been returned to God thus it came from his soul in a state of sleep within his blood.

Job's Expectation

Job 19:25-26

> For I know that my Redeemer lives and He shall stand at last on the earth: And after my skin is destroyed, this I know, that in my flesh I shall see God ...

This well known verse appears at just about the middle of the book of Job and, as is the pattern in many other books of the Bible, is a turning point verse. It has been the subject of endless debate because Job claims that "*in my flesh I shall see God*" whereas this is seemingly contrary to Paul's statement in 1 Corinthians 15:50 "*flesh and blood cannot inherit the kingdom of God ... etc*" The translators have had a difficult time with this verse. Interestingly, there is a variant reading given as a footnote to verse 26 in the NIV that reads, "*And after I awake, I shall see God ...*" As far as is known, the Conditionalists do not use this variant reading to support their position but it does so nicely and that may be one reason for all the debate.

Jarius' Daughter

Matthew 9:24

> He [Jesus] said to them, "Make room, for the girl is not dead, but sleeping [*katheudo*]." And they laughed Him to scorn.

Jesus used the Greek word *katheudo* meaning natural sleep yet He had been told (v.18) that the girl had just died. In the case of Lazarus [See below, John 11:11-14] He used the word *koimaomai*, but the reason for His choice of the word *katheudo* for Jarius' daughter is not clear.

Raising of Lazarus.

John 11:11-14

> These things He said, and after that He said to them,
> "Our friend Lazarus sleeps [*koimaomai*], but I go that I
> may wake him up." Then His disciples said, "Lord, if he
> sleeps [*koimaomai*] he will get well." However, Jesus spoke
> of his death, but they thought that He was speaking about
> taking rest in sleep [*hupnos*]. Then Jesus said to them
> plainly, "Lazarus is dead."

John 11: 26

> [Jesus] And whoever lives and believes in Me shall never die.
> Do you believe this?

We saw earlier that the Greeks had three words that meant sleep: *katheudo* that most often meant normal sleep, *koimaomai* that meant the resting or sleep of death and *hupnos* that always meant normal voluntary sleep. The text spells out quite clearly that the disciples had mistaken Jesus' meaning by His use of the word *koimaomai* and assumed that He meant *hupnos*, or normal sleep. So when Jesus said, "Lazarus *koimaomai* [sleeps]," He was saying that Lazarus was resting and He meant dead and finally said so. If He had meant Lazarus was in normal sleep He would have used the word *hupnos*. We can be sure that Jesus chose His words carefully and was teaching us a truth if we are open to receive it. From God's viewpoint this account and others is saying that death is only a special kind of deep sleep, sometimes referred to as "involuntary sleep" to distinguish it from normal or "voluntary sleep." Further, this is not likely to be referring to the body since given sufficient time this completely disappears. Thus, most reasonably, it is referring to the soul. With regard to Jesus' statement that the Believers "*shall never die*" (John 11:26), so far, every believer in Christ has died physically or will do so, yet Jesus would not lie. He was, of course, referring to the second death in this statement while at the same time telling us that something still lives, the *vestigium vitae*, after our first [natural] death.

Jesus to the Repentant Thief

Luke 23:42-43.
> [Jesus] I say to you, today you will be with me in Paradise.

The objections pointed out for the use of this passage to defend the immortal soul position are essentially those very points used to defend the Conditionalist position. In other words, Jesus clearly was not in paradise that same day and, as we shall see from "Paul's mystery" below, Jesus was not only telling the thief but also the reader that time stands still for the dead. The Conditionalist sometimes makes the defense that since there was no punctuation in the original text, it is quite legitimate to place the comma after the word "today"—"*I tell you today,* ..." but this is a strained and unnecessary argument.

Paul's "Mystery"

Paul's mystery that "we shall all be changed in a moment, in a twinkling of an eye, at the last trumpet" refers to the Second Coming and includes those Believers who are still alive and those who are in their graves.

1 Corinthians 15:50-52
> Now this I say, brethren, that flesh and blood cannot inherit the kingdom of God; nor does corruption inherit incorruption. Behold, I tell you a mystery; we shall not all sleep [*koimaomai*], but we shall all be changed—in a moment, in the twinkling of an eye, at the last trumpet. For the trumpet will sound, and the dead will be raised incorruptible, and we shall be changed.

1 Thessalonians 4:13-17
> But I do not want you to be ignorant, brethren, concerning those who have fallen asleep [*koimaomai*] ... even so God will bring with Him those who sleep [*koimaomai*] in Jesus. [But] we who are alive and remain until the coming of the Lord will by no means precede those who are asleep [*koimaomai*]. For the Lord Himself will descend from heaven with a shout, with the voice of an archangel, and with the trumpet of God. And the dead in Christ will rise first. Then those who are alive and remain shall be caught

up together with them in the clouds to meet the Lord in the air.

Conditionalists recognize that Paul's *"twinkling of an eye"* not only describes what will be experienced by the resurrected dead but will also be experienced a few moments later by the righteous living as they change to the glorified body. For example, the thief on the cross will experience two millennia of gravedom as *"the twinkling of an eye"* and to him it will be *"this day."* Once it is understood that time stands still for the dead just as it does in a good night's sleep, many Christians concede that the perceived difference between the Conditionalist position and the Immortal Soul position pales to insignificance. Those of the Conditionalist position readily concede that to the individual, death will be experienced as a fleeting moment immediately followed by the trumpet and "going straight into the arms of Jesus."

The early writings of Calvin lack the balanced approach of the mature mind and in his latter years he came to see that the Anabaptist "heresy" of soul sleep was more perceived than real. Luther had never waivered from the Conditionalist position and this was one of the points of contention between Calvin and Luther. Many notable scholars have openly questioned the doctrine of the immortal human soul. Froom gives a long list of scholars who openly adopted the Conditionalist position including such well-known names as Paul Tillich and Karl Barth. Fudge[4] lists a number of others including : B. R. Reichenbach and H. Thielicke (Lutherans), A. A. Hoekema and D. G. Bloesch (Calvinists) and F. F. Bruce (Brethren). Some, such as the Seventh Day Adventists, openly reject neo-platonism and teach the Conditionalist view. Increasingly, many others today in the mainline churches, both pastors and laymen, have also come to accept the Conditionalist view although they are often reluctant to speak of it openly. However, there remains this important difference between the two teachings: Teaching Conditional Immortality supports the doctrine of the resurrection whereas teaching Innate Immortality tends to deny it.

Conclusion

Prior to the nineteenth century, before Darwin, before the teaching of liberal theology and before the introduction of cremation, the importance of the general resurrection was emphasized in both sermon and song. For example, the Nicene Creed was put to music by

J. S. Bach in his *Credo of the Mass* in B Minor while the high point of this performance is *"the resurrection of the dead."* Or again, in Handel's *Messiah* the song of triumph appears at the end with Paul's expectation of the general resurrection when *"the last trumpet shall sound and we shall be changed."* We have seen in previous chapters many of the subtle ways in which the importance of the resurrection has been diminished. While there are undoubtedly other subtle detractions yet one more can be mentioned. The word "rapture" replaced the words "caught up" 1 Thessalonians 4:17 at some time in the late 1800's. Paul did not use the word "resurrected" for *"the living who remain"* but the word *harpazo* which is correctly translated as "caught up" or "snatched away." This tells us that, like Enoch and Elijah, those last-day Believers will not die, thus will not be resurrected, but their mortal body will instantly change to the glorified body. The words "caught up" more readily convey to the reader what will happen on that wonderful day of the Second Coming than the more obscure word "rapture."

We have seen in previous chapters that there are a number of verses in Scripture that many would agree have caused division within Christendom. It was also pointed out that articles of faith are not based upon proof but upon evidences. This is true for the interpretation of origins in nature as it is for the interpretation of Scripture. As in a court of law, we can only weigh the evidences. When approached objectively, putting aside popular teaching and carefully reading in full context, it is believed that the original intended meaning of Scripture can be resolved. We have tried to do this in these chapters. The conclusion appears to be that inspired Scripture has been given to us in such a way that we have a choice. On the one hand, we can take the broad road and subscribe to Satan's lying promise of immortality. On the other hand and with a little more diligence, we can weave our narrow way through some admittedly difficult verses and gain a more secure understanding of the destiny of the soul and the gift of eternal life from our loving Saviour.

11

Vestigium Vitae

To be blessed in death, one must learn to live.
To be blessed in life, one must learn to die.

DUPLESSIS-MORNAY (1549–1623)
FRENCH HUGUENOT LEADER

Life in the Dead?

The early Christians used the Latin v*estigium vitae* or "vestige of life" when referring to certain phenomenon in the recently dead. We have already seen Scripture's use of the word "sleep" to indicate a vestige of life in mortal death. This may be reflected in the Greek word for memorial grave, *mnemeion*, meaning a place to preserve the memory or where memories are preserved. The counterpart Hebrew word, *Beth-haim*, is more positive and means "house of the living."

We saw earlier that not only the Hellenized Jews but many other cultures around the world have a belief that for a few days after natural death there is still some "life" in the corpse. The Egyptians, the Greeks and some Jews for example believed that the soul lingered about the body for three days. The Muslims believe it is forty days. The Jews refer to the body as the *goses* immediately before death but following the final death rattle—believed to be the expulsion of God's spirit—the body, now a corpse, is referred to as a *peger*. The Greeks had the word *pethamenos* for a recently dead body but later, when in decay, it was referred to as *nekros*. *Pethamenos* means that while dead, it still has the potential to return to life and in this sense is similar to the Hebrew *goses*. It is likely that these two terms were used because of the difficulty in determining the actual point of death; those rare cases where someone has been declared "dead" only to revive again and perhaps live for several more years would certainly help to sustain this uncertainty.

The early Church father, Tertullian, although a believer in the immortal soul wrote in his *De Anima*, "*Death separates the soul from the body, although some have supposed that in certain cases souls still have adhered to the body after death ..."* [1] Throughout Christian literature there are a number of accounts of miraculous movements of the dead. For example, there is the case of the 16th century martyr who just before he was beheaded, told his persecutors that they would see a miracle to prove that while they could destroy his body, they could not destroy his soul. The headless body lying on the ground then crossed its hands and feet.[2] Apart from the obvious miracles, there are two possible explanations for movement in the recently dead body: The first is based upon Scriptural interpretation and the second upon a naturalistic explanation. As we have seen before, we can make a freewill choice of the interpretation we wish to accept. The Scriptural interpretation makes an appeal to the business at Elisha's grave and to the words of Paul:

2 Kings 13:20-21
> ... and they put the [dead] man in the tomb of Elisha;
> and when the man was let down and touched the bones
> of Elisha, he revived and stood on his feet.

1 Corinthians 15:36-38
> Foolish one, what you sow is not made alive unless it dies.
> And what you sow, you do not sow that body that shall be,
> but mere grain—perhaps wheat or some other grain. But
> God gives it a body as He pleases, and to each seed its own
> body.

To use Paul's analogy, a seed that is planted consists mostly of food for the "germ" that is present within the seed. That "germ" contains the DNA or genetic blueprint for the new plant. This genetic information directs the molecules of water, minerals etc. from the ground to become that new plant. The germ in the seed is thus alive and the new plant looks something like the old one that "died."[3] Paul gave us this analogy in his first letter to the Corinthians above and seemed to have this same analogy in mind when he wrote his second letter to the Corinthians:

2 Corinthians 1:21-22
> Now He who establishes us with you in Christ and has
> anointed us is God, who also has sealed us and given us
> the Spirit in our hearts as a deposit.

2 Corinthians 5:5

> Now He who has prepared us for this very thing is God, who also has given us the Spirit as a guarantee [downpayment, earnest]

Ephesians 4:30

> And do not grieve the Holy Spirit of God, by whom you were sealed for the day of redemption.

The Conditionalist teaching uses Paul's analogy of the germ in the seed to refer to the sleeping soul that resides together with Christ's Spirit as a "deposit" in the earth. That sleeping soul is the "pattern or blueprint" for the new body and, if the analogy of the seed is still valid, it will not use the same atoms that were in the original body.

Another source of the belief in the *vestigium vitae* is the strange feeling that many people experience at the funeral home. A close relative, and especially a long time spouse, will often report that the "presence" of the dead can be strongly felt for the first day or so then, often on the third day, that "presence" has gone. This is a purely subjective experience for which there can be no proof but it is common enough. While there seems to be no Scripture for this experience it does tend to reinforce the belief that the soul is conscious and separable. On the other hand, Scripture does tell us that God knows our days and, for those sensitive to His leading, many have testified to having known a short time before the day of their departure. God is a God of order and it would seem entirely within His character to graciously lets us know when to put our house in order. Perhaps in a similar way, by the experience of the removal of that "presence" in the funeral home, the loved one left behind is given assurance that departure is final. It is time to return the body to the earth.

For those who prefer the naturalistic explanation for the *vestigium vitae,* several can be offered to explain why this almost universal belief exists. One obvious explanation is that a patient may be incorrectly diagnosed as dead when in fact he is in a deep coma. Later recovery, or especially claims of recovery after burial, have led to fears among the living of premature burial. We were introduced to some of these horror stories in Chapter Four. Medical authorities assure us that most of these stories are entirely untrue and there is very little chance of this happening today. On the other hand, medical science still has no way of establishing the exact moment of death. However, once *rigor mortis* has set in and decay follows, gases do build up in the body cavity causing body movements and even posthumous flatus. Even during cremation there can be quite violent body movements due to exploding gas. The Roman naturalist Pliny the Elder provides a long and somewhat tedious catalogue of purported movements of the dead. However, at this point in time there is no way of verifying these accounts but no doubt there was a perfectly natural explanation in most cases.

Viewing the Dead

Christians often ask if it is right to have an open casket at the funeral home? God has given us Scripture to inform us just sufficiently that we may be protected from that evil spirit world about us. For example, most Christians will acknowledge we should have nothing to do with witchcraft or attempting to contact the dead. At the same time, there are a number of other verses that tell us that touching the dead or even coming near the dead can cause us to be defiled or unclean:

Numbers 19:11
> He who touches the dead body of anyone shall be unclean seven days.

Numbers 19:16
> Whoever in the open field touches one who is slain by a sword or who has died, or a bone of a man, or a grave, shall be unclean seven days.

Ezekiel 44:25
> They [the priests] shall not defile themselves by coming near a dead person.

It is sometimes argued that these rules were for those of the Old Testament and do not apply to the Christian today. However, this is exactly the attitude that the Father of Lies would encourage. While the Christian is protected by the blood of Jesus we are expected to exercise wisdom and caution. Missionaries and anthropologists of the nineteenth century reported that throughout the pagan world the dead body was always believed to be saturated with danger for mortals and thus generally regarded as taboo.[4] Those who had to handle the dead for disposal were reckoned to be defiled for a number of days and certain cleansing exercises were necessary. All this is found in the Old Testament but may even then be dismissed as superstition except for the fact that well documented cases have been, and are still being, reported in Christian countries. Just three cases will be given here:

1) Thomas H. Huxley, a surgeon, an agnostic and the good friend of Charles Darwin, told how his elder brother had taken him at the age of 14 years (1839) to see a dead body. He wrote that it was a psychological shock that almost killed him. He believed—for the rest of his life—that he had somehow been poisoned by the sight and "from that time on my constant friend, hypochondrical dyspepsia, commenced this half century of contenancy [sic]."[5]

2) An American patient, referred to as Eve White, was taken at the age of 5 to see her dead grandmother in her coffin and her mother insisted that she touch the face of the corpse. The girl was terrified and her problems began to manifest themselves coming to a head in 1952 when she was found under psychiatric examination to be a triple personality. This was unusual at the time but these personalities were willing to be filmed and the resulting film *The Three Faces of Eve—a study of multiple personality* has circulated among the medical schools for decades.[6]

3) Peter Sutcliffe began employment at the age of 18 in 1964 digging graves at Bingley cemetery in northern England. He was a lapsed Catholic, opened coffins and stole from the dead and began to hear voices from the graves. In 1967 he claimed that God had told him that he was on a divine mission to kill prostitutes. By that time he had murdered thirteen women.[7]

While the medical profession diagnosed Sutcliffe as a paranoid schizophrenic this does not explain in a satisfactory manner what was going on. However, when demon possesion is considered, then all the facts for the Sutcliffe case and for Eve White nicely fall into place. It is not being suggested here that T.H.Huxley was possessed. Clearly, not every person who dies is possessed but of those few who are, it would seem reasonable to believe that the evil spirit would seek to inhabit another body. Traditions such as touching the dead and especially kissing the dead justified by Genesis 50:1—could terrify a person, especially a child, and provide the precise opportunity for the spirit to transfer from the dead to the living.

Peter Sutcliffe, aged about 19, employed as a grave-digger. He boldly opened coffins to steal rings etc. from the dead, then began to hear voices and finally the voice of "God" telling him to murder prostitutes. [London Express News Service, UK.]

Stepping on a Grave

There are several verses that warn us that stepping on a grave causes defilement:

Numbers 19:16

Whoever in the open field ... touches one who has died,
or a bone of a man, or a grave, shall be unclean seven days.

Luke 11:44

Jesus: "Woe to you, scribes and Pharisees, hypocrites!
For you are like graves which are not seen, and the men
who walk over them are not aware of them."

Except for the most pagan societies who dispose of their dead via the birds or as ashes, civilized societies have always marked the burial place of their dead. It may be a monument or a simple wooden marker but the purpose is two-fold: Firstly, that the relatives know where they have laid their dead and secondly, to serve as a warning to others not to step on the grave-site. During the past century, the church-yards of the older churches have became filled then closed while the new churches tend to be built in urban areas and there is no church-yard. The public cemeteries have slowly taken over the business of body disposal and are organized and businesslike. There are strict regulations regarding record-keeping and maintainance while the burial plots are usually very well marked. In short, stepping on a grave today usually requires a deliberate effort.

Charles Darwin's grave is an interesting exception: He died in April 1882 and was buried in the floor of the north aisle of Westminster Abbey, near Sir Isaac Newton. The stone covering his grave forms part of the floor. A few years ago when it was decided to charge visitors a fee to enter the inner part of the Abbey, a turn-stile was installed in the choir screen just at the foot of Darwin's grave. This was assuredly not done with deliberate intention but it has caused every paying visitor to walk the length of Darwin's grave and thus, according to Numbers 19:16, be unclean for seven days!

Each of the Gospels of Matthew, Mark and Luke contain the account of the Gadarene demoniac—the man possessed by a legion of evil spirits and who lived in the tombs.

Mark 5:2-3

>   ... immediately there met Him [Jesus] out of the tombs
>   a man with an unclean spirit, who had his dwelling
>   among the tombs ...

While the account does not specifically state that the man became possessed while living in the tombs this may be inferred. Moreover, there have been reported historical cases even into the present day. There is the well-known legend of the Christian hermit, Paphnutius, who tried to convert the beautiful courtesan, Thäis, to Christianity. He finished up insane with unsatisfied lust and ran off to live in a tomb where he became possessed by the voices from the stone floor. During the past century Thäis has been produced as a play, as a book by Anatole France and as an opera but the story is based upon an account traceable back to the fifth century. In 1983 an article reported in *Psychology Today* dealt with the problem of teen-age legend-tripping.[8] Legends often surround certain graves and these become popular drinking sites for adolescents; the graves are usually heavily vandalized. The case is cited of the grave of Mary Jane who was alleged to be a witch thus not buried in the church cemetery while the curse associated with the grave was supposedly responsible for two teen-age deaths. There will likely never be a solidly identifiable cause and effect in these cases yet cemetery authorities, police and psychiatric hospitals are well aware that teen-age thrill seekers involved with grave sites or tombs often finish up traumatized or with a personality change.

Charles Darwin's grave in the North aisle floor of Westminster Abbey. Thousands of visitors walk on this gravestone every year as they pay to enter at the turn-stile. [Photo by author]

Phantom Limb

For all but the victim, this is a strange phenomenon. When a limb is lost, say in battle or amputated, the victim can often feel pain in distal parts of the missing limb, that is, the fingers in the case of an arm. The pain persists to the patient's last day. Nerve-blocking drugs are employed to alleviate the discomfort but usually with limited success. There is often a measure of truth in folklore and tradition and the older literature records some insight into this problem although no naturalistic explanation. It was said that in times of battle both sides would set aside a day to clear the battlefield of the dead and severed limbs to ensure decent burial. The records made it clear that the limbs especially required burial to ensure the absence of pain in the victim-survivors. In 1981 Casetta and Thiederman recorded 28 accounts of amputated limbs which had to be buried in order to prevent the phantom limb pain. Sometimes the limb had to be exhumed in order to straighten it out while occasionally the orientation was important.[9]

This writer has personally interviewed a retired Pentecostal pastor who had lost four fingers from his left hand in an accident as a teenager. He related that the pain in the missing fingers was severe for almost a year after the accident, then the missing fingers were discovered and given a decent burial. From that moment and for

THE GREATEST GIFT OF ALL
IS TO GIVE ONESELF
FOR OTHERS

WE HERE COMMEMORATE
SUCH GIFTS TO ALL
MANKIND THROUGH THE
ADVANCEMENT OF SCIENCE

North American hospitals and anatomy schools at one time returned all amputated limbs and parts used for teaching to the earth in special burial plots in the public cemetery. Not so today. [Courtesy: University of Waterloo]

the next fifty years he had never felt the pain again. This may be dismissed as mere anecdote and there is certainly no natural explanation but is it just because there is no naturalistic explanation that these accounts are dismissed? If so, this is surely not the spirit of true scientific inquiry! In 1986 a paper appeared in a periodical specifically devoted to those who had lost limbs and challenged the medical profession. It was suggested that the medical community carry out a simple statistical test to monitor the method of limb disposal and the incidence of phantom limb pain to see if there is any correlation.[10] As far as is known, no work of this kind has ever been conducted although the cost would be minimal. However, if the correlation is positive the possible benefits to future amputees would be enormous. It is certainly significant that until about 1960 most hospitals in North America had a place at the local cemetery where amputated limbs were buried. In the last few decades, however, disposal of all body parts at North American hospitals has been by incineration and phantom limb pain is a continuing problem for patients. The exceptions are the Jewish hospitals that are still very careful to ensure that every amputation or organ removed is identified and kept that it may eventually accompany its owner to the cemetery. For others facing the prospect of amputation and not having access to a Jewish hospital, it may be helpful to know that there is a legal requirement in most jurisdictions that the patient be offered the option of burial or incineration for disposal of the limb.[11]

This chapter has been written to offer some further insight into those aspects of departure and place of departure that could not easily be included in the check-list style of the final chapter.

—o◯o—

12

Getting Ready for Departure

Beneath those rugged elms, that yew-trees shade,
Where heaves the turf in many a mould'ring heap,
Each in his narrow cell for ever laid,
The rude forefathers of the hamlet sleep.

THOMAS GRAY, *ELEGY* ... 1750

Becoming Familiar With the Rules

Better to Bury than to Burn has been written especially for those in the Christian community who need answers to the cremation question and believe that Scripture is the Word of God. In North America there are laws that make it mandatory for each body disposal to be handled through a registered funeral establishment. A body cannot be buried just anywhere. Further, in most places the funeral establishment must be a separate organization from the cemetery company. These laws were put in place for the protection of the public, although very often the cemetry and the funeral establishment have a cosy relationship. The following suggestions are intended as a guide to those who wish to depart in a way that will honor God's commandment to return to the dust of the ground. This book has been written at a time when the individual in North America still has the option of being buried or cremated. Unless the Christian Church wakes up, we may find that in the not too distant future that option will not be available. Listed below are some reasonable recommendations to consider before departure:

1. While there is no law of the land that requires the use of a coffin, or casket, most cemeteries have by-laws that forbid the entry to the cemetery grounds of any dead body that is not properly contained. Further, since it must be handled by the funeral staff they usually prefer a rigid container. In the normal way, this would seemingly leave no option and the family are left to purchase the wooden or metal casket. Increasingly today they are persuaded

116

to also purchase a concrete vault to cover the casket. The concrete is said to prevent slumping or subsidence of the ground as the unprotected casket eventually rots away. All this is unscriptural, unnecessary and should be vigorously resisted. The industry does produce special cardboard containers although these are seldom, if ever, offered as an option.[1] There will be no slumping with the cardboard container. If the funeral establishment cannot, or will not, offer one of these containers ask them to order one. It can be stored in its flattened condition in a dry place at home if necessary. If all else fails, the thinest of chipboard containers that will collapse under the weight of soil will be suitable. The cemetery is the first place to make inquiries.

2. Well ahead of time, be sure to cultivate trustworthy Christian friends who are younger than yourself. At least two such friends will be necessary as executors and they need to be mature enough to ensure that your requests are carried out. At the time of writing the law still says that a body cannot be cremated unless a specific request has been made. Conversely, the body must be buried if specifically requested. Discuss this with your attorney when making your will as the day may be near when laws are passed to make cremation mandatory.

3. Why not patronize the Christian community and use the services of a Christian funeral establishment? Not all can be recommended of course, so it is a good idea to consult your pastor or priest who probably knows who is who in the local funeral business.

4. Make a visit to the recommended establishment and discuss your needs with one of their representatives. This can be done years ahead of time and there is usually no charge for consultation and no commitment necessary.

5. Embalming is not a legal necessity unless the body is going to be shipped out of Province or out of State. Only in this case does the law require that the body be embalmed to retard decomposition and safeguard other travellers during transportation. If the body must be shipped and embalmed, discuss with the funeral establishment if it would be possible to have the blood transferred to a sealed container that accompanies the body. When the body is lowered to its final resting place the contents of the container should then be emptied into the grave.

6. The open casket for viewing the dead—especially kissing the dead—is an utterly pagan custom and Christians should have no part of it. On rare occasions when two people of the same name die on the same day, mortuaries have made mistakes. It is therefore a wise precaution to have a mature and close relative identify the body before closure. Scripture and Christian custom indicate defilement of the priest by seeing a dead body. Children and even teenagers should not be allowed to see the dead as this could cause life-long psychological problems.

7. Virtually all amputations today are incinerated. When entering a hospital for an operation that may involve amputation, every patient has the option of specifying the means of disposal. While this is usually not offered because most patients never ask, be quite insistent that the limb or other body part, is properly identified and given decent burial. Folklore usually contains an element of truth. It will cost nothing to take this precaution and may avoid years of pain.

8. Should a Christian give a blood donation? The soul is the "life in the blood" but a blood donation does not cause loss of the donor's life. There would seem to be no problem in giving "the gift of life," a blood donation. Receiving a blood transfusion raises the question that if the soul is divisible then the transfused blood will contain part of another person's soul. This is at the root of some religious objections to blood transfusion. Scripture does not seem to be specific on this issue and it is suggested that each individual take Paul's advice to do whatever the Spirit is saying for their particular circumstances but do not make a divisive issue of it with others.

9. Should a Christian donate organs after decease? The orthodox Jew will not do this because it means that that part of his body may not return to the dust of the ground. The recipient may, for example, be cremated or the organs never implanted in a donor but finish forgotten in storage and later incinerated. In other words, there is no control over the donated organs once they have been harvested. It might be wise therefore to politely leave this type of charitable donation to the pagan world.

10. Finally, the grave should be in a spot where it will not be disturbed. Of course, this can never be guaranteed but if proper

earth burial has been carried out there should be no trace of the body left after say, ten years. The marker might be a simple empty cross with a brief scripture to proclaim the resurrection. Why not, "Sleeping in Jesus"?

Appendix A

The Comfortable Words of the Good Bishops

In the light of all that Scripture has to say regarding body disposal and the underlying stress placed upon returning to the earth, not in one Scripture verse but in many, we thought it might be interesting to see what Church of England Bishops have had to say about cremation. We are reminded that these men have had a long academic training in some of the finest universities that Britain has to offer and have been schooled in the original languages of Scripture. The British Cremation Society solicited their opinions some years ago and published the following statements with their approval.

Rt. Rev. William D. L. Greer
(Anglican Bishop of Manchester, 1947–1970):

"… in the first place it [cremation] *seems to me to be entirely in accord with Christian teaching when rightly understood. Secondly, it will lead to a great saving of land, and as time goes on will become of increasing importance."*

Rt. Rev. Edward F. Moore
(Anglican Bishop of Armagh, Ireland, 1959–):

"There is no theological objection to cremation, so that method of disposal of a dead body is an acceptable alternative to burial."

Rt. Rev. Clement G. Parker
(Anglican Bishop of Bradford, 1961–1972):

"While it is important to retain freedom of choice, I am anxious to support the extensive use of the practice of cremation. I see no theological reason against this method of disposal."

Rt. Rev. James Frazer
(Anglican Bishop of Manchester, 1870–1886):

> *"... no intelligent faith can suppose that any Christian doctrine is affected by the manner in which or the time in which this mortal body of ours crumbles to dust."*

Rt. Rev. Henry R. McAdoo
(Anglican Bishop of Ossory, Ireland, 1962–1977):

> *"I am sure that there can be no theological objection whatever to the practice of cremation."*

Rt. Rev. Robert W. Jackson
(Anglican Bishop of Limerick, Ireland, 1960–):

> *"There are, of course, no theological reasons which would give preference to burial as against cremation."*

Rt. Rev. Robert C.H. Elliot
(Anglican Bishop of Armagh, Ireland, 1956–1969):

> *"I am thankful for the increasing use of cremation ... I am convinced that there is nothing contrary to Christian Religion in the reverent reduction of our mortal remains to ashes, in place of the long, drawn-out process of decay occasioned by earth burial."*

Rt. Rev. Ronald R. Williams
(Anglican Bishop of Leicester, 1953–1979):

> *"Religious objections have long ceased to be felt generally in the Church of England, but there will always be those who prefer the symbolism of burial, and such views must be treated with consideration and respect."*

Appendix B

Man was made from the dust of the ground

Genesis 18:27

Abraham speaking: "I who am but dust [*epher*] and ashes [*aphar*]"
Abraham was using an expression that nicely rolled off the Hebrew
tongue and was not implying that Adam was made from a pre-adamic ash
heap! Note the slightly different phonetic spelling for dust and for ashes;
this difference results from the different Hebrew final letter and the
pointing.

Job 4:19

... those who dwell in houses of clay, whose foundation is in the dust.

Job 10:9

You have made me like clay and will You turn me into dust again?

Job 34:15

If He should gather to Himself His Spirit and His breath, all flesh
would perish together, and man would return to dust.

Psalm 90:3

You turn men back to dust, saying, "Return to dust, O sons of of men."

Psalm 103:14

For He knows our frame; He remembers that we are dust.

Psalm 104:29

You take away their breath, they die and return to their dust.

Ecclesiastes 3:20

All go to one place: all are from the dust, and all return to dust.

Ecclesiastes 12:7

Referring to human death: Then the dust will return to the earth as it was,
and the spirit will return to God who gave it.

1 Corinthians 15:47-49

The first man was of the earth, made of dust;
As was the man of dust, so also are those who are made of dust;
And as we have borne the image of the man of dust.

The Earth is in the feminine gender

Genesis 4:11

... the earth [*adamah*], which has opened its mouth to receive ...

Numbers 16:30

... and the earth [*adamah*] opens its mouth and swallows them up

Numbers 16:32
> ... and the earth [*erets*] opened its mouth and swallowed them up

Numbers 26:10
> ... and the earth [*erets*] opened its mouth and swallowed them up

Deuteronomy 11:6
> ... how the earth [*erets*] opened its mouth an swallowed them up

Isaiah 61:11
> For as the earth [*erets*] brings forth its bud, as the garden causes

Ezekiel 34:27
> ... and the earth [*erets*] shall yield her increase.

Jonah 2:6
> The earth [*erets*] with its bars closed behind me forever;

Mark 4:28
> For the earth [Gk. *ge*] yields crops by itself

James 5:18
> And he prayed again ... and the earth [Gk. *ge*] produced its fruit.

The first use of a word in Scripture is recognized to be important since the context usually defines its meaning. The first two usages of the word *adamah* [earth] placed it in the feminine gender and the older KJV consistently used "her" in reference to the earth throughout the translation. Modern translators, including the NKJV above, have tried to depart from the archaic appearance of "her" and have used "its" but have not been consistent. As may be seen above the original word translated as "earth" has not been consistent either: initially feminine [*adamah*] then masculine [Hebrew *erets* and in the Greek *ge*. The feminine Greek is *Gaia*].

Placing oneself under the dust

Joshua 7:6
> ... both he and the elders of Israel; and they put dust on their heads.

I Samuel 4:12
> Then a man of Benjamin ... with his clothes torn and dirt on his head.

2 Samuel 1:2
> ... a man came from Saul's camp with ... dust on his head.

2 Samuel 15:32
> Hushai the Archite ... with his robe torn and dust on his head.

Nehemiah 9:1
> ... the children of Israel ... and with dust on their heads.

Job 2:12
> each one tore his robe and sprinkled dust on his head

Lamentations 2:10
> The elders of the daughter of Zion ... throw dust on their heads.

Ezekiel 27:30
> They will cry bitterly and cast dust on their heads;

Revelation 18:19.
> And they threw dust on their heads and cried out ...

Both man and beast each have a spirit [*ruach*]

Genesis 6:17
> ... destroy all flesh in which is the breath of life [*ruach*]

Genesis 7:15
> ... all flesh in which is the breath of life [*ruach*]

Genesis 7:22
> ... all in whose nostrils was the breath of the spirit of life [*ruach*]

Job 12:7-10
> ... the beasts ... the birds ... the fish ... the Lord in whose hand is the life [*nephesh*] of every living thing, and the breath [*ruach*] of all mankind.

Job 33:4
> The Spirit [*ruach*] of God has made me, and the breath [*neshamah*] of the Almighty gives me life [*chayah*].

Psalm 104: 29-30
> You take away their breath [*ruach*], they die and return to their dust. You send forth Your Spirit [*ruach*], they are created and You renew the face of the earth.

Acts 17:28
> for in Him we live and move and have our being, as also some of your own poets have said, "For we are also His offspring."

Sacrificial blood must be returned to the ground

Exodus 24:6
> And Moses took half the blood [of oxen] and put it in basins, and half the blood he sprinkled on the altar.
> [Moses was seemingly heavy-handed with the blood but the full details of the practice of the sacrifice had not yet been given].

Exodus 29:16
> ... kill the ram, ... take its blood and sprinkle it around on the altar

Exodus 29:20
> ... and sprinkle the blood [of a ram] all around on the altar.

Leviticus 1:5
> He shall kill the [young] bull ... and sprinkle the blood all around on the altar, that is, by the door of the tabernacle of meeting.

Leviticus 1:11
> ... slaughter it ... shall sprinkle its blood all around on the altar.

Leviticus 3:2
>... shall sprinkle the blood all around on the altar.

Leviticus 3:8
>... shall sprinkle the blood all around on the altar

Leviticus 3:13
>... shall sprinkle the blood all around on the altar

Leviticus 4:7
>shall pour the remaining blood of the bull at the base of the altar ...

Leviticus 4:18
>pour the remaining blood at the base of the altar of burnt offering ...

Leviticus 4:25
>and pour its blood at the base of the altar of burnt offering.

Leviticus 4:30
>and pour all the remaining blood at the base of the altar.

Leviticus 4:34
>and pour all the remaining blood at the base of the altar.

Leviticus 5:9
>the blood shall be drained out at the base of the altar.

Leviticus 7:2
>And its blood he shall sprinkle all around on the altar.

Leviticus 8:15
>... and he poured the blood at the base of the altar ...

Leviticus 8:19
>Then he sprinkled the blood all around on the altar.

Leviticus 8:24
>Moses sprinkled the blood all around on the altar.

Leviticus 9:9
>... and poured the blood at the base of the altar.

Leviticus 9:12
>... the blood which he sprinkled all around on the altar.

Leviticus 9:18
>... the blood which he sprinkled all around on the altar

Leviticus 17:6
>... the priest shall sprinkle the blood on the altar ...

Leviticus 17:13-14
>And whatever man ... catches an animal or bird that may be eaten,
>he shall pour out its blood and cover it with dust; for it is the life of
>all flesh. Its blood sustains its life ... for the life of all flesh is its blood.

Non-burial regarded as posthumous punishment.

Deuteronomy 28:26

Moses warning the people the consequences of not obeying the Lord:
"Your carcasses shall be food for all the birds of the air and the beasts of
the earth, and no one shall frighten them away."

1 Samuel 17:46

David to Goliath:
"... And this day I will give the carcasses of the camp of the Philistines
to the birds of the air and the wild beasts of the earth, that all the earth
may know that there is a God in Israel."

2 Samuel 4:12

So David commanded his young men, and they executed them [Rachab
and Baanah], cut off their hands and feet, and hanged them by the pool
in Hebron.

1 Kings 14:11

The prophet Ahijah to King Jeroboam's wife:
"The dogs shall eat whoever belongs to Jeroboam and dies in the city,
and the birds of the air shall eat whoever dies in the field; ..."

2 Kings 23:16

And he [Josiah] sent and took the bones out of the tombs and burned
them on the altar, and defiled it according to the word of the Lord ...

Jeremiah 16:4

The Lord to Jeremiah concerning the people of Jerusalem:
"They shall die gruesome deaths; they shall not be lamented nor shall
they be buried, but they shall be like refuse on the face of the earth.
They shall be consumed by the sword and by famine, and their corpses
shall be meat for the birds of heaven and for the beasts of the earth.

All life is received from God

Numbers 16:22

O God, the God of the spirits [*ruach*] of all flesh.

Ecclesiastes 12:7

and the spirit [*ruach*] will return to God who gave it.

Zechariah 12:1

... the Lord who ... forms the spirit [*ruach*] of man within him:

Hebrews 12:9

... be in subjection to the Father of spirits [*pneuma*] and live?

James 2:26

For as the body without the spirit [*pneuma*] is dead,
so faith without works is dead also.

Man is born a sinner

Job 14:1-4

Man who is born of woman is of a few days and full of trouble.
… And do You … bring me to judgment with Yourself?
Who can bring a clean thing out of an unclean?

Psalm 51:5

David: Behold I was brought forth in iniquity,
And in sin my mother conceived me.

Psalm 58:3

The wicked are estranged [delivered] from the womb;
They go astray as soon as they are born, speaking lies.

2 Peter 2:12

But these, like natural brute beasts made to be caught and destroyed,
speak evil of the things they do not understand, and will utterly perish
in their own corruption.

Jude 10

But these [the dreamers] speak evil of whatever they do not know;
And whatever they known naturally, like brute beasts, in these things
they corrupt themselves.

The frequency of use of the word "sleep" to mean death.

Hebrew	radam	Used 6 times meaning sleep as in a trance, never death
	shakab	Used 49 times meaning death and burial 40 times
	shena	Used 24 times meaning death 2 times.
	yashen	Used 24 times meaning death 4 times
Greek	hupnos	Used 6 times meaning normal sleep, never death
	katheudo	Used 21 times meaning death 3 times
	koimaomai	Used 17 times meaning death 13 times

Sleep means death

Acts 7:60

The stoning of Stephen:
And when he had said this he fell asleep [koimaomai]

1 Corinthians 15:51

I tell you a mystery: We shall not all sleep [koimaomai],
but we shall all be changed—in a moment,
in the twinkling of an eye, at the last trumpet.
For the trumpet will sound, and the dead will be raised
incorruptible, and we shall be changed.

1 Thessalonians 4:13-14

But I do not want you to be ignorant, brethren,
concerning those who have fallen asleep [koimaomai],

lest you sorrow as others who have no hope.
For if we believe that Jesus died and rose again,
even so God will bring with Him those who sleep [*koimaomai*] in Jesus.

Our destiny is the grave

Psalm 7:5

NKJV: [David] And lay my honor in the dust.
NIV: [David] And make me sleep* in the dust.
[* *yashen* is not in the original and the verse has difficulties]

Psalm 13:3

Consider and hear me O Lord my God; enlighten my eyes,
lest I sleep [*yashen*] the sleep [*yashen*] of death;

Psalm 115:17

The dead do not praise the Lord, nor any who go down into silence.

Ecclesiastes 9:5-6

For the living know that they will die; but the dead know nothing,
... Nevermore will they have a share in anything done under the sun.

Ecclesiastes 9:10

Whatever your hand finds to do, do it with your might;
for there is no work or device or knowledge or wisdom
in the grave[*sheol*] where you are going.

Spontaneous Human Combustion

Numbers 11:1-3

So the fire of the Lord burned among them [the Israelites],
and consumed some in the outskirts of the camp.

2 Kings 1:7-15

Elijah orders fire to come down from heaven to consume
the king of Samaria's fifty men.

Ezekiel 28:18-19.

The Lord speaking through Ezekiel to the king of Tyre:
"I brought fire from your midst; it devoured you,
and turned you to ashes upon the earth ..."

—— o◯o ——

Bibliography

ADAMS, Norman. 1972. *Dead and Buried: The Horrible History of Body Snatching.*
Aberdeen, UK.: Impulse Books.

ALTHAUS, Paul. 1975. *The Theology of Martin Luther* translated by R. C. Schultz.
Philadelphia: Fortress Press

ARIÈS, Philippe. 1991. *The Hour of Our Death* translated by Helen Weaver.
Oxford: Oxford University Press.

ARNOLD, Larry E. 1995. *Ablaze: Spontaneous Human Combustion.*
New York: M. Evans & Co.

ARUNDEL, Lord of Wardour. 1872. *Tradition.*
London: Burns, Oates & Co.

AUGROS, Robert & George Stanciu.1987. *The New Biology*
Boston: New Science Library

BAILEY, James Blake. 1896. *The Diary of a Resurrectionist, 1811-1812.*
London: Swan Sonnenschein.

BANNER, Hubert S. 1934. *These Men were Masons.*
London: Chapman and Hall.

BENDANN, E. 1930. *Death Customs*
London: Kegan Paul, Trench, Trubner & Co.

BERGENGREN, Erik. 1962. *Alfred Nobel*
London: Thomas Nelson & Son

BEVERIDGE, Henry (translator). 1957. *Institutes of the Christian Religion by John
Calvin.* Grand Rapids, MI: William B. Eerdmans. 2 vols.
Reprint of 19th century ed.

BEVERIDGE, Henry (translator). 1958. *Tracts and Treaties in Defense of the Reformed
Faith by John Calvin.* Grand Rapids, MI: William Eerdmans. 3 vols.
Reprint of 1851 ed.

BIGELOW, Allen Gilman. 1886. Cremation and Christianity.
The North American Review (New York) October Vol. 143, p. 353-359.

BOND, Peter. 1967. The Celebration of Death.
Architectural Review (London) April Vol. 141, p.303

BRACEGIRDLE, Cyril. 1987. *Doctor William Price: Saint or Sinner?*
London: Whitaker Press.

BUDGE, E.A. Wallace. 1971. *Egyptian Magic*
    New York: Dover Publications reprint.

BURN, Gordon. 1984. *Someone's Husband, Somebody's Son: The Story of Peter Sutcliffe*
    London: William Heinemann

BUTCHER, S. H. and Andrew Lang. 1887. *The Odyssey of Homer.*
    London: Macmillan.

CAMERON, Charles. 1887. The Modern Cremation Movement.
    The Scottish Review (London), July 10:1-38.

CATHCART, William. 1989. *The Papal System.*
    Watertown, WI: Baptist Heritage Press. Reprint of 1872 ed.

CLARK, Ronald W. 1968. *The Huxleys*
    London: Heinemann

COBB, Augustus G. 1882. Earth Burial and Cremation.
    The North American Review (New York), September, 135:266-282.

COLE, Hubert. 1964. *Things for the Surgeon: A History of the Resurrection Men.*
    London: Heinemann.

COLGRAVE, B. and R.A.B. Mynors (editors). 1969. *Bede's Ecclesiastical History ...*
    Oxford: Clarendon Press

CROCKFORD'S Clerical Directory 1977-1979.
    London: Oxford University Press. 87th issue

CROWELL, John R. 1979. Invasion of the Body Snatchers
    Law Enforcement Communications (New York) April, Vol. 2 (2), p.8-9

CURL, James S. 1972. *The Victorian Celebration of Death*
    London: David & Charles.

DIODORUS Siculus. 1700. *The Historical Library of Diodorus the Sicilian in
    Fifteen Books done into English* (Translator not given).
    London: Printed by Edward Jones for Awnsham and Churchill.

DODS, Marcus. 1903. *Forerunners of Dante.*
    Edinburgh: T. and T. Clark.

DODS, Marcus (translator). 1950. *The City of God by Saint Augustine.*
    New York: Random House.

DUEK, Lorna. 1991. Dream Turned Fact Launches Best Selling Author.
    Christian Week (Winnipeg, MB), June 11.

EASTON, A. M. and K. G. V. Smith. 1970. The Entomology of the Cadaver.
    Medicine, Science and the Law (Beaconsfield, UK), 10:208-215.

ELLIS, Bill. 1983. Adolescent Legend-Tripping
    Psychology Today (Washington), August, 17:68-69.

EVANS, W. E. D. 1963. *The Chemistry of Death.*
    Illinois: Charles C. Thomas.

FAUCIEUX, A. 1886. La Crémation.
    Revue des Sciences Ecclésiastiques (Paris) 6th ser. 4:481

FOX, John. 1967. *Fox's Book of Martyrs.* Grand Rapids, MI: Zondervan

FRAZER, Sir James George. 1918. *Folk-Lore in the Old Testament.*
    London: Macmillan. 3 vols.

FRAZER, Sir James George. 1920. *The Golden Bough. Part III, The Dying God.*
    London: Macmillan. 3rd edition, 12 vols.

FRAZER, W.M. 1950. *A History of English Public Health, 1834-1939*
    London: Baillière, Tindall and Cox

FROOM, LeRoy Edwin. 1966. *The Conditionalist Faith of Our Fathers.*
    Washington, DC.: Review and Herald. 2 vols.

FUDGE, Edward William. 1982. *The Fire that Consumes.*
    Houston, TX.: Providential Press.

GARDINER, Eileen. 1989. *Visions of Heaven and Hell before Dante*
    New York: Italica Press

GASPERARRI, Pietro. 1939. *Codis juris canonici fontes.*
    Rome: 9 vols. Quote translated by R. McDougal S.J.

GEBHARD, Bruno. 1976. The Interrelationships of Scientific and Folk Medicine in
    the U.S.A. In: *American Folk Medicine: A Symposium Edited by Wayland Hand*
    CA.: University of California Press.

GIBSON, Walter S. 1973. *Hieronymus Bosch*
    New York: Praeger Publishers

GORINI, Paolo. 1876. *Sulla purificazione dei morti per mezzo del fuoco*
    Milan: Lodi, printer of pamphlet. Translated by R. McDougal S.J.
    British Museum Catalogue # 7391 f.5

GRANT, A.J. (editor) 1897. *Herodotus: Rawlinson's Translation.*
    New York: Charles Scribner's Sons. 2 vols.

GREENE, Leon. 1997. If I Should Wake Before I Die
    Wheaton, IL: Crossway Books

GRIFFITH, John. 1995. Smoke Scheme
    New Scientist (London) January 14, Vol. 145, p.48

HASTINGS, James. 1921. *Encyclopedia of Religion and Ethics.*
New York: Charles Scribner's Sons. 13 vols.

HENGEL, Martin. 1977. *Crucifixion.* Translated by John Bowden
Philadelphia: Fortress Press.

HIEBERT, D. Edmond. 1971. *The Thessalonian Epistles.*
Chicago: Moody Press.

HIND, Henry Youle. 1863. *Explorations in the Interior of the Labrador Penisular*
London: Longman Green

HOLMES, Peter (translator). 1870. De Anima—A Treatise on the Soul.
In: *The Writings of Quintus Septiminuis Tertullianus.*
Edinburgh: T. and T. Clark.

IRION, Paul E. 1968. *Cremation.*
Philadelphia: Fortress Press

JEBB, Richard (translator). 1957. *The Tragedies of Sophocles.*
Cambridge: Cambridge University Press.

JOWETT, B. (translator). 1937. *The Dialogues of Plato.*
New York: Random House. 2 vols. Reprint of 1892 ed.

KEIL, C. F. and F. J. Delitzsch. 1983-84. *Commentary of the Old Testament
in Ten Volumes, Translated from the German.*
Grand Rapids, MI: William B. Eerdmans Publishing Co.
Reprint of 19th century ed. in 10 vols.

KROLL, Jerome and B. Bachrach. 1982. Visions and Psychopathology in the
Middle Ages. *Journal of Nervous and Mental Disease.* Vol. 170, p. 41-49.

KROPOTKIN, Peter. 1971. *The Great French Revolution* translated by N. F. Dryhurst
New York: Schocken Books. Reprint of 1910 edition.

LECLERCQ, M. 1969. *Entomology and the Medical Sciences.* Oxford:
Pergamon Press.

LYALL, Alfred C. 1899. *Asiatic Studies, Religious and Social*
London: John Murray. 2 vols.

McGINN, Bernard. 1979. *Visions of the End: Apocalyptic Traditions in the Middle Ages*
New York: Columbia University Press.

MELLARS, P. and C. Stringer. 1989. *The Human Revolution: Behavioral Perspectives
in the Origins of Modern Humans.*
Princeton: Princeton University Press

MITFORD, Jessica. 1963. *The American Way of Death.*
New York: Simon & Schuster.

MORE, Henry. 1647. *A Platonic Song of the Soul.* Issued in various parts:
    Immortality of the Soul; Confutation of the Sleep of the Soul, etc.
    Note: More's name does not appear on this poetic publication.
    Cambridge: Printed by Roger Daniel, printer to the University.

MORTON, Samuel George. 1839. *Crania Americana*
    Philadelphia: J. Dobson

NEWMAN, Alfred. 1893. Cremation
    The Westminster Review (London) June Vol. 139, p. 654-659

PATAI, Raphael. 1972. *Myth and Modern Man.*
    Englewood Cliffs, NJ: Prentice-Hall

PRICE, Douglas B. 1981. Miraculous Restoration of Lost Body Parts: Relationship
    to the Phantom Limb Phenomenon and to Limb Burial Superstitions and
    Practices. In: *American Folk Medicine: A Symposium.* Wayland D. Hand, ed.
    University of California Press, Berekeley. 3 vols. See pages 49-71

REIER, Sharon. 1978. All Sales Are Final
    Forbes Magazine (New York), October 30, p.106-108

SABOM, Michael B. 1982. *Recollections of Death: A Medical Investigation.*
    New York: Harper and Row.

SALTER, W.H. 1970. *The Society for Psychical Research: An Outline of its History*
    London: 1, Adam & Eve Mews, W8

SCHAMA, Simon. 1989. *Citizens: A Chronicle of the French Revolution*
    New York: Alfred A. Knopf

SHEN, T. and S. Liu. 1953. *Tibet and the Tibetans*
    California: Stanford University Press

SLACK, Kenneth. 1984. Lightning and "Heresy" at York Minster.
    The Christian Century (Chicago), 101:787.

SLACK, Kenneth. 1985. Durham: The Saga Continues.
    The Christian Century (Chicago), 102:437

SPENCER, Stewart and B. Millington. 1993. *Wagner's Ring of the Nibelung*
    London: Thames & Hudson

STANNARD, R.W. 1958. A Churchman's View of the Growing Practice of
    Cremation. *Church Times* (London) September 19, Vol. 141, p.11

STEVENSON, James. 1978. *The Catacombs.*
    Nashville, TN: Thomas Nelson Publishers

STRONG, Augustus H. 1969. *Systematic Theology.*
    Old Tappan, NJ: Fleming H. Revell Co., 3 vols. in 1.

TAYLOR, Ian. 1986. Phantom Limb Pain: A Challenge to the Medical Profession.
   The Fragment (Ottawa), Fall, 150:24-26.

TEGG, William. 1876. *The Last Act.*
   London: William Tegg and Co.

THIGPEN, C. H. and H.M. Cleckley. 1957. *The Three Faces of Eve*
   Kingsport, TN: Kingsport Press, Inc.

THOMPSON, Sir Henry. 1874. Cremation· A Reply to Critics.
   The Contemporary Review (London), 23:553.

THOMPSON, Sir Henry. 1889. *Modern Cremation, Its History and Practice.*
   London: Kegan Paul. Reprints in 1891, 1899, 1901 etc.

TYLOR, Sir Edward Burnett. 1970. *Religion in Primitive Culture.*
   Gloucester, MA. Peter Smith.
   Reprint of 2nd edition of *Primitive Culture,* 1873.

TRITT, Michael.L. 1974. *The Motif of Premature Burial in the Tales of Edgar Allan Poe*
   MA thesis, McGill University. National Library, Ottawa.
   AMICUS # 000067458

WALSH, M.B. 1967. Cremation
   New Catholic Encyclopedia (New York) Vol. 4, p. 441

WARMINGTON, E. H. editor. 1969. *Natural History in Ten Volumes of Pliny the Elder.*
   London: Heinemann. Reprint.

WEISHEIPL, James A. 1974. *Friar Thomas D'Aquino: His Life, Thought and Work.*
   New York: Doubleday.

WHISTON, William. 1985. *The Works of Josephus.*
   Peabody, MA: Hendrickson Publishers. Reprint of 1804 ed.

WHITE, Andrew D. 1978. *A History of the Warfare of Science with Theology in
   Christendom.* Gloucester, MA: Peter Smith. 2 vols. Reprint of 1896 ed.

WOODWARD, K. L. 1985. Britain's Doubting Bishop.
   Newsweek (New York) June 17, 105:91

YADIN, Yigael. 1985. *The Temple Scroll.*
   London: Weidenfeld and Nicolson.

—— o◯o ——

References

Chapter 1. How Cremation was Introduced

1. Welsh Revival. There were at least eight revivals from 1735 in each of which about10% of the population was converted. The most memorable were 1857 and 1904.
2. Bracegirdle 1997
3. Shen & Liu 1953, 150
4. Augros & Stanciv 1987, 117
5. Kropotkin 1902, 34
6. Crowell 1979, 6:8
7. Easton & Smith 1970, 10:208
8. Leclercq 1969, 128
9. Evans 1963, 40
10. Mitford 1963, 196
11. Pliny's *Natural History*, Book 7, 54:187 In: Warmington 1969, 633
12. During the Vietnam War the Americans always buried their dead, friend or foe. However, the Vietcong buried only their own and would deliberately burn or mutilate enemy bodies. Usually heads were severed and scattered from the bodies. For this reason, the local Vietnamese often chose to join the Vietcong to avoid mutilation and be sure of a decent burial.
13. Homer's *Iliad*, Book 24, lines 770-804 In: Lang 1883, 502
14. Virgil's *Aeneid*, Book 11, lines 203-224 In: Lonsdale 1910, 247.
15. Yadin 1985, 183
16. Stevenson 1978, 24
17. Mozart had joined the "Zur Wohltätigkeit" [Through Charity] Masonic Lodge in Vienna as No. 20 on the lodge register on December 14, 1784. He wrote *The Magic Flute* in 1791 and in this opera exposed some of their rituals. By this time he was also in debt to several of his Masonic brethren. Whe he died in 1791, Masonic funeral honors were not extended to him even though he had written the Masonic funeral music [Kv. 477] still used at Masonic funerals today. Further, because he had become a Mason, he was also refused the Roman Catholic burial rites. He was given a pauper's burial at St. Marx's cemetery.
18. Curl 1972, 28.
19. At the celebrated "iron coffin case" of 1821 the judge made his deliberation on the fact that iron would occupy burial space for a much longer period of time than traditional wood and therefore a surcharge for the use of the ground should be applied. For the really curious see: *English Law Reports* Vol. 161, p.761-773.
20. Tegg 1876, 368
21. Kropotkin 1971, 520-523
22. Schama 1989, 777-778
23. Cameron 1887, 10: 6
24. Frazer 1950, 66. This is an account of the infamous case of the Broad Street pump in central London that led to hundreds of deaths from cholera via the ground water.

25. Cameron 1887, 9
26. Weisheipl 1974, 330ff
27. Ball 1928, 46
28. Cole 1964, 88
29. Cole 1964, 106ff
30. Adams 1972, 8
31. Gebhard 1976, 90
32. Bailey 1896, 88

Chapter 2. The Continuing Conspiracy

1. Thompson 1874, 23: 319 – 328, 553 – 571
2. Those in Sir Henry Thompson's little group were:
   Sir Thomas Spencer Wells, surgeon to Queen Victoria;
   Sir John Everett Millais, portrait painter to royalty;
   Sir John Tenniel, illustrator for Punch magazine and books
   including the Rev. Dodgson's *Alice in Wonderland*;
   Shirley Brooks. Charles William Shirley Brooks, always known as Shirley Brooks
   was editor of Punch magazine and contributor to periodicals. Initiated as
   member of St. Thomas's Masonic Lodge, London, on June 25, 1844.
   Anthony Trollope; employee of British Post Office, traveller for the PO and
   novelist. He was initiated into the Masonic Lodge of the Irish Constitution on
   November 8, 1841.
   Frederick A. Lehmann; German-born, naturalized Briton. Partner in the US
   Steel company, Naylor-Vickers, at the time of the American Civil War
   (1861-65). He became very wealthy.
3. Bigelow 1886, 143:353
4. Newman 1893, 139: 654
5. Cameron 1887, 10:1,6,9
6. Irion 1968, 77. From: *Pharos* (UK) 1962, 28: 23
7. Walsh 1967, 4:441 in *New Catholic Encyclopedia*
8. Irion 1968, 78
9. Banner 1934, 235
10. Gorini 1876
11. Mackay and McClenachan 1924, 2: 621
12. Gasparri 1886 referenced in Walsh 1967, 441
13. Faucieux 1886, 508
14. Faucieux 1886, 509
15. Crockford's, 1977-79, 868 under "Robinson"
16. Woodward 1985, 105:91
17. Slack 1984, 101:787; 1985, 102:437
18. Reier 1978, 106

Chapter 3. Attacking the Resurrection

1. Budge 1971, 63
2. Morton 1839, 244
3. Arundel 1872, 309

4. Bendan 1930, 281
5. Hind 1863, 1:170
6. Plato, *Republic* In: Jowett 1937, 1: 591 [lines given in text]
7. Plato, Timaeus In: Jowett 1937, 2: 3
8. Plato, *Phaedrus* In: Jowett 1937, 1: 233
9. Plato, *Laws* In: Jowett, 1937, 2: 407
10. Plato, *Phaedo,* In: Jowett 1937, 1: 465
11. There are a number of well-known Christian evangelists who by their writings
    have promoted the idea in the Church of pre-adamite man. Alexander
    Winchell's *Pre-adamites* first published in 1880 went through five printings and
    not only promoted pre-adamite man but blatantly racist ideas. Winchell was
    professor of geology at the University of Michigan and a professing Christian.
    Among others who bowed to Winchell's word as the scientist were:
    Congregational evangelist R.A.Torrey, Pentecostals Kathryn Kuhlman
    and Derek Prince and Anglican Dr. John Stott.
12. Augustine, *City of God* 8: 4 In: Dods 1950, 247
13. Augustine, *City of God* 6: 12 In: Dods 1950, 205
14. Calvin, *Tracts & Treaties...* In: Beveridge 1958, 3: 414-418
15. More 1647
16. Hastings 1921, 11: 428

Chapter 4. Some of the More Subtle Methods

1. Tylor, 1970, 140
2. The International Association for Near Death Studies. In: Sabom 1982, 184
3. Greene, 1997
4. Duek, June 11, 1991 p.8-9 The death certificate is not mentioned in her books
   but she does mention it in her spoken testimony. See also Greene 1997, 49-51.
5. Tertullian, *De Anima,* 9 In: Holmes 1870, 2: 426
6. Augustine, *City of God,* 20: 25 and 21: 21 In: Dods 1950, 753, 791
7. Bede's *Ecclesiastical History* 5:12 In: Colgrave 1969, 489
8. Dods, 1903, 208
9. Kroll 1982, 170:41 Analysis of 134 Visions Reported in the Middle Ages.
   See also: McGinn 1979 and Gardiner 1989 for more Medieval visions.
10. Virgil, *The Aeneid* 6: 724 In: Lonsdale & Lee, 1910, 174
11. Gardiner, 1989
12. Gibson, 1973, 57. Hieronymus Bosh painted his famous *Ascent of the Blessed,* the
    tunnel of light, as the second of a pair of painted panels or wings, one on each
    side of the high altar in the Palace of the Doges, Venice, about 1490. Tundale
    had had the tunnel experience centuries earlier, but the legend in an early
    writing was finally published in Holland in 1484. The story inspired Bosch
    and graphically served to inspire many thousands of others since. It has
    the church's blessing and thus seemingly has the authority of Scripture.
    The second panel was a scene of the terrestrial paradise [Eden].
13. Flannery, 1988, 1: 63
14. Roth, 1892, 151; White, 1896, 2: 52 and O'Malley, 1964, 64
15. Ives 1984, 346
16. Stannard, September 19, 1958, 141:11
17. Tritt 1974

18. Bergengren 1962, 177
19. Griffith 1995, 145:48
20. Typical book title: *One Thousand Buried Alive by their Best Friends* by M. R. Fletcher published in Boston, 1890.
21. Salter 1970, 6
22. *Encyclopedia Britannica*, 11th ed. 1910, 25:705. A very long and detailed article of the history of spiritualism by E. M. Sidgwick, secretary of the Society for Psychical Research but, of course, no mention of the Fox sisters confession of fraud. This was given by Margaretta and Leah Fox and reported by a series of articles in the *New York Herald* on September 24, October 9 and 22, 1888
23. Just a few names of SPR members: Edward Benson White, later Archbishop of Canterbury; Lord Rayleigh, the physicist; Alfred Russel Wallace the co-discoverer with Charles Darwin of natural selection; Sir William Crookes, later President of the Royal Society; Arthur Balfour, later prime minister of England and author of the famous Balfour Agreement; Rev. C.L. Dodgson, better known as Lewis Carroll author of *Alice in Wonderland*; Sir Leslie Stephen, father of Virginia Woolf; John Ruskin, art critic.
24. Irion 1968, 81
25. Bond, 1967, 141:303

Chapter 5. The Life is in the Blood

1. As an interesting aside, the lower rib bones are the only bones in the human body that re-grow when a small piece has been removed for surgery provided the protective sheath (periosteum) has not been removed. While the number of human rib bones can vary, males do not consistently have one less rib bone than females.
2. Frazer 1918, 1:3-29
3. Frazer 1918, 1: 9-11
4. Keil 1983, 1: 4:122

Chapter 6. Defiling the Land

1. Some commentators believe the reason we ask the Lord to bless the food before we eat it is to remove the effect of the curse that was pronounced upon the ground in Genesis 3:17.
2. Keil 1983, 9: 1:343
3. Sophocles, lines 450-459 In: Jebb 1957, 141
4. Diodorus Book 1, Chap.6
5. Frazer 1920, Part 3, 42
6. Frazer 1920, Part 4, Vol.1: 124, 174, 176, 181
7. Frazer 1920, Part 3, 43
8. Lyall 1899, 2:314
9. Patai 1972, 279 Also in: Frazer 1920, Part 3, 42
10. Spencer 1993, 351
11. Arnold 1995
12. Hengel, 1977, 24
13. Holmes 1870, 2:533

Chapter 8. Origin and Destiny of the Soul

1. Calvin's *Psychopannychia* In: Beveridge 1958, 3: 420
2. Calvin's *Institutes'* 1: 15: 2 In: Beveridge 1957, 1: 160
3. Heibert 1971, 253

Chapter 9. But What Do the Scriptures Say?

1. Josephus "Extract from Discourse" In: Whiston 1985, 637 and 714

Chapter 10. What is Conditional Immortality?

1. Ariès 1991, 24
2. Althaus 1975, 414
3. Josephus In: Whiston 1985, 637 and 714
4. Fudge 1982, 409

Chapter 11. Vestigium vitae

1. Tertullian Book 2:51 In: Holmes 1870, 2: 523
2. Fox 1967, 173
3. When seeds are kept too long before planting they will fail to reproduce, and thus will have "died" indicating that prior to this they were "alive."
4. Bendann 1930, 84
5. Clark 1968, 10
6. Thigpen 1957. Earlier reported in C.H.Thigpen and H.Cleckley *Journal of Abnormal and Social Psychology.* 1954, 49:135-151
7. Burn 1984
8. Ellis 1983, 17: 69
9. Casetta A. & Thiederman, B. In: Hand 1981, 2: 300
10. Taylor 1986, 150: 24
11. Court of Appeals of Kentucky, file W-182-72. Re: KRS 311.352
    Should legal difficulties arise, the legal precedent for the right to have amputated limbs buried have been set by this case.

Chapter 12. Getting Ready for Departure

1. The following are Canadian wholesale and retail suppliers of cardboard and chipboard containers in business at the time of writing:

   Wholesale: Northern Caskets, P. O. Box 326, Lindsay, Ontario K9V 4S3. Tel: 1-800-461-1428. While they do not sell directly to the public they do supply funeral homes in Canada and distribute throughout the US.

   Retail: Public Casket Sales, 327 Eglinton East, Toronto, ON. M4P 1L7 Tel: 416-440-3299

—— o◯o ——

Index

A

Abel, 2

Abraham's bosom, 91

Achan cremated as added punishment, 69

Acts 13:48 quoted, 94; 17:26 quoted, 78; 22:23 partial quote, 54; 26:5-8 quoted, 93

Adam and Eve, 78, 79; not immortal, 34

Adam created from dust, 24, 83, 99; created in perfection, 54, 57; still sleeps, 97; the Fall of, 81, 84; Adam's rib and modern surgery, 139(5-1)

Adipocere, 5

Advent, the first, 28

Alexandria, Greek colony, 28; Jews, 29

Altars of Noah and Abram, 58

American Civil War, 14

Amos 6:10 quoted, 68

Amputated limbs and pain, 114, 118

Anabaptists defined, 32, 105; Anne Hendriks burned, **33**

Anatomy Act, 14; Anatomy schools, 12, 13

Anglican Church, position on soul sleep, 98

Animal Kingdom not fallen, 57

Annulment of marriage, 91

Apostles' Creed, 24, 37, 98

Aquinas, Thomas, 12; and indulgences, 44

Archbishop Runcie, of Church of England, 22

Ariès, Philippe, quoted, 97

Aristotle as Plato's student, 27

Ascent of the Blessed, painting, 42; details, 138(4-12)

Ash Wednesday, the imposition, 46

Ashes to ashes, not Scriptural, 45

Athanogoras introduces neo-platonism, 30

Atonement sacrifice, meaning of, 57, 58, **59**

Augustine praises Plato, 30; establishes neo-platonism, 30; portrait of, **31**; quotes 1 Corinthians 3:12-15, 40; promotes purgatory, 42

B

Babylonian legend of creation of man, 55

Bacon, Francis, *Novum Organum* quoted, 74; on bias, 74

Basket coffin, 4, 8

Bede, The Venerable, 41

Benson, E.W., Archbishop, 50, portrait, **51**

Bier, not coffin, 6

Blake, William, neo-platonist, 28, **29**

Blessing the food, 139(6-1)

Blood hastens decay process, 5; sustains life, 5; returned to the ground, 58, 59, 60; blood donations, 117

Bosch, Hieronymus, 42

Brooks, Shirley, portrait, **16**; details, 137(2-2)

Browne, Thomas, quoted, 2, 54

Browning's *Epistle of Karshish,* 90

Buddhists reporting trips to heaven, 40

Burial of limbs to avoid pain, 114, **115**

Burial prayer, ashes to ashes, 45

Burke and Hare, Resurrection men, 13

C

Cadavers for anatomy schools, 14

Calvin, John, portrait, **31**; against Anabaptists, 32; dichotomist/neo-platonist, 82, 105; *Institutes,* quoted, 82, 83

Cambridge neo-platonists, 32

Casket manufacturers, 140(12-1)

Catacombs, 6, 7

AGMV Marquis

MEMBER OF SCABRINI MEDIA

Quebec, Canada
2002